CROCHETED
WILD ANIMALS

CROCHETED
WILD ANIMALS

A collection of woolly friends to make from scratch

Vanessa Mooncie

The Taunton Press

The Taunton Press
Inspiration for hands-on living®

The Taunton Press, Inc., 63 South Main Street
P.O. Box 5506, Newtown, CT 06470-5506
e-mail: tp@taunton.com

First published 2013 by
Guild of Master Craftsman Publications Ltd
Castle Place, 166 High Street, Lewes,
East Sussex, BN7 1XU

Library of Congress Cataloging-in-Publication
Mooncie, Vanessa.
  Crocheted wild animals : a collection of wild and woolly friends
to make / Vanessa Mooncie.
     pages cm
  Includes bibliographical references and index.
  ISBN 978-1-62113-990-4 (paperback)
1. Crocheting--Patterns. 2. Soft toy making. 3. Stuffed animals
(Toys) I. Title.
  TT829.M66 2013
  746.43'4--dc23
                    2013029351

Publisher: Jonathan Bailey
Production Manager: Jim Bulley
Managing Editor: Gerrie Purcell
Senior Project Editor: Wendy McAngus
Editor: Nicola Hodgson
Managing Art Editor: Gilda Pacitti
Design: Rob Janes/Simon Goggin
Photographer: Andrew Perris
Charts and technique illustrations: Vanessa Mooncie

Set in Frutiger
Color origination by GMC Reprographics

Printed and bound in the United States of America

Where those wild animals roam

The animals

Techniques

Introduction

This colorful collection of crocheted animals is aimed at both adults and children. The projects featured are suitable for both adventurous beginners and advanced crafters and are all fun to crochet as an ideal keepsake or gift.

The projects are crocheted mainly in DK (CYCA 3) yarns; your choice of colors and textures can be varied to create a unique piece of work. The majority of the projects are worked in rounds or rows of single crochet; details such as markings and feathers are usually worked separately and may feature other crochet stitches.

The individual character of each animal is defined by its features. You can make the animals as cute and friendly or as fierce and ferocious as you like, simply by changing the size and position of the eyes on the face.

Buttons and beads are used in some of the projects, but the eyes can be worked in French knots or crocheted discs instead if the animal is intended for babies or young children.

Many of the designs of these wild animals were inspired by illustrations found in old children's books. Starting off with just a couple of balls of yarn and a crochet hook, you can create a fascinating creature from scratch with a unique story of its very own.

Vanessa Mooncie

Fabulous flamingo

Sensational snake

Marvelous monkey

Funny frog

Curvaceous camel

Divine deer

Elegant elephant

Fantastic fox

Cool chameleon

Gorgeous giraffe

The animals

Crocheted entirely in one shade of camel-color yarn,
this sleepy dromedary looks as if he would be happy to bask
all day long in the desert sun given half a chance.

Camel

ONE HUMP OR TWO?

A camel with two humps is called a Bactrian, while this camel is a Dromedary because he has only one.

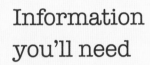

Information you'll need

Finished size
Approximately 9¼in (23.5cm) tall (not including the ears)

Materials
Rico Design Essentials Merino DK (or equivalent DK weight yarn, CYCA 3), 100% merino wool (131yds/120m per 50g ball)
2 x 50g balls in 054 Camel (A)
C/2–D/3 (UK11:3mm) crochet hook
Darning needle
Toy stuffing
Air-erasable fabric marker or tailor's chalk pencil
Embroidery needle
Stranded embroidery thread in black

Gauge
22 sts and 24 rounds to 4in (10cm) over single crochet using C/2–D/3 hook

Key

⊙ Wind yarn around finger to form a ring

• Slip stitch (sl st)

∂ Chain (ch)

+ Single crochet (sc)

x͟x 2 sc in same st

ʌ͟x sc2tog

x͟ʌ͟x 3 sc in same st

⟊ Single crochet into back loop only

⟊ Slip stitch into the back loop of
single crochet and chain at the
same time to join

How to make Camel

The camel is worked in single crochet throughout. The body is crocheted in continuous rounds; the hump is shaped by increasing and then decreasing stitches over the length of the top of the back. The neck is continued from the body, but worked in rows rather than rounds. Increasing the center stitches and decreasing the stitches at the edges forms the curve in the neck. The head and the legs are crocheted in continuous rounds. The ears are made up of two identical pieces, each worked in rows and then joined by crocheting the last row of each piece together at the same time. The camel is finished with a tasseled tail and embroidered features.

Head

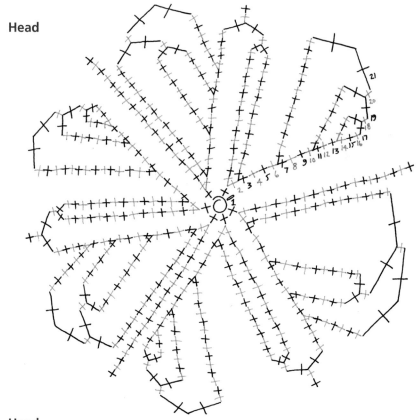

Head

Starting at the tip of the nose, with C/2–D/3 hook and A, wind yarn around a finger a couple of times to form a ring, insert the hook, catch the yarn, and draw back through the ring.

Round 1: 1 ch (does not count as a st), work 6 sc into ring (6 sts).

Round 2 (inc): (2 sc in next sc) 6 times (12 sts). Pull on short end of yarn to close ring.

Round 3 (inc): (2 sc in next sc, 1 sc) 6 times (18 sts).

Rounds 4–6: Work 1 sc in each sc.

Round 7 (inc): (2 sc in next sc, 2 sc) 6 times (24 sts).

Rounds 8–10: Work 1 sc in each sc.

Round 11 (inc): (2 sc in next sc, 3 sc) 6 times (30 sts).

Rounds 12–13: Work 1 sc in each sc.

Round 14 (inc): (2 sc in next sc, 4 sc) 6 times (36 sts).

Rounds 15–16: Work 1 sc in each sc.

Shape back of head

Round 17 (dec): (Sc2tog, 2 sc) 9 times (27 sts).

Round 18: Work 1 sc in each sc.

Round 19 (dec): (Sc2tog, 1 sc) 9 times (18 sts).

Round 20: Work 1 sc in each sc.

Round 21 (dec): (Sc2tog, 1 sc) 6 times (12 sts).

Fasten off, leaving a length of yarn and thread through the last round of stitches, stuff the head firmly, gather up the opening and stitch to secure.

Body

Starting at the tail end, with C/2–D/3 hook and A, wind yarn around a finger a couple of times to form a ring, insert the hook, catch the yarn and draw back through the ring.

Round 1: 1 ch (does not count as a st), work 6 sc into ring (6 sts).

Round 2 (inc): (2 sc in next sc) 6 times (12 sts). Pull on short end of yarn to close ring.

Round 3 (inc): (2 sc in next sc, 1 sc) 6 times (18 sts).

Round 4 (inc): (2 sc in next sc, 2 sc) 6 times (24 sts).

Round 5 (inc): (2 sc in next sc, 3 sc) 6 times (30 sts).

Round 6 (inc): (2 sc in next sc, 4 sc) 6 times (36 sts).

Round 7 (inc): (2 sc in next sc, 5 sc) 6 times (42 sts).

Shape hump

Round 8: Work 1 sc in each sc.

Round 9 (inc): 1 sc in next 19 sc, 2 sc in next sc, 2 sc, 2 sc in next sc, 19 (44 sts).

Round 10 (inc): 1 sc in next 20 sc, 2 sc in next sc, 2 sc, 2 sc in next sc, 20 sc (46 sts).

Round 11 (inc): 1 sc in next 21 sc, 2 sc in next sc, 2 sc, 2 sc in next sc, 21 sc (48 sts).

Round 12 (inc): 1 sc in next 22 sc, 2 sc in next sc, 2 sc, 2 sc in next sc, 22 sc (50 sts).

Round 13 (inc): 1 sc in next 23 sc, 2 sc in next sc, 2 sc, 2 sc in next sc, 23 sc (52 sts).

Round 14 (inc): 1 sc in next 24 sc, 2 sc in next sc, 2 sc, 2 sc in next sc, 24 sc (54 sts).

Round 15 (inc): 1 sc in next 25 sc, 2 sc in next sc, 2 sc, 2 sc in next sc, 25 sc (56 sts).

Round 16 (inc): 1 sc in next 26 sc, 2 sc in next sc, 2 sc, 2 sc in next sc, 26 sc (58 sts).

Round 17 (inc): 1 sc in next 27 sc, 2 sc in next sc, 2 sc, 2 sc in next sc, 27 sc (60 sts).

Rounds 18–24: Work 1 sc in each sc.

Round 25 (dec): 1 sc in next 27 sc, sc2tog, 2 sc, sc2tog, 27 sc (58 sts).

Round 26 (dec): 1 sc in next 26 sc, sc2tog, 2 sc, sc2tog, 26 sc (56 sts).

Body
Rounds 1–24

Body
Rounds 24–34

Round 27 (dec): 1 sc in next 25 sc, sc2tog, 2 sc, sc2tog, 25 sc (54 sts).
Round 28 (dec): 1 sc in next 24 sc, sc2tog, 2 sc, sc2tog, 24 sc (52 sts).
Round 29 (dec): 1 sc in next 23 sc, sc2tog, 2 sc, sc2tog, 23 sc (50 sts).
Round 30 (dec): 1 sc in next 22 sc, sc2tog, 2 sc, sc2tog, 22 sc (48 sts).
Round 31 (dec): 1 sc in next 21 sc, sc2tog, 2 sc, sc2tog, 21 sc (46 sts).
Round 32 (dec): 1 sc in next 20 sc, sc2tog, 2 sc, sc2tog, 20 sc (44 sts).
Round 33 (dec): 1 sc in next 19 sc, sc2tog, 2 sc, sc2tog, 19 sc (42 sts).
Round 34: Work 1 sc in each sc.

Shape neck

The following is worked in rows:
Row 1 (dec): Sc2tog, 17 sc, (sc2tog) twice, 17 sc, sc2tog, turn (38 sts).
Row 2: 1 ch (does not count as a st), work 1 sc in each sc, turn.
Row 3 (dec): 1 ch (does not count as a st), sc2tog, 15 sc, (sc2tog) twice, 15 sc, sc2tog, turn (34 sts).
Row 4: 1 ch (does not count as a st), work 1 sc in each sc, turn.
Row 5 (dec): 1 ch (does not count as a st), sc2tog, 30 sc, sc2tog, turn (32 sts).
Row 6: 1 ch (does not count as a st), work 1 sc in each sc, turn.
Row 7: 1 ch (does not count as a st), sc2tog, 13 sc, (2 sc in next sc) twice, 13 sc, sc2tog, turn.
Row 8: 1 ch (does not count as a st), work 1 sc in each sc, turn.
Row 9: As row 7.
Row 10 (dec): 1 ch (does not count as a st), sc2tog, 28 sc, sc2tog, turn (30 sts).

Row 11: 1 ch (does not count as a st), sc2tog, 12 sc, (2 sc in next sc) twice, 12 sc, sc2tog, turn.
Row 12 (dec): 1 ch (does not count as a st), sc2tog, 26 sc, sc2tog, turn (28 sts).
Row 13: 1 ch (does not count as a st), sc2tog, 11 sc, (2 sc in next sc) twice, 11 sc, sc2tog, turn.
Row 14 (dec): 1 ch (does not count as a st), sc2tog, 24 sc, sc2tog, turn (26 sts).
Row 15: 1 ch (does not count as a st), sc2tog, 10 sc, (2 sc in next sc) twice, 10 sc, sc2tog, turn.
Row 16 (dec): 1 ch (does not count as a st), sc2tog, 22 sc, sc2tog, turn (24 sts).
Row 17: 1 ch (does not count as a st), sc2tog, 9 sc, (2 sc in next sc) twice, 9 sc, sc2tog, turn.
Row 18: As row 17. Do not turn at the end. Fasten off, leaving a long length of yarn at the end.

Shape neck
Rows 1–18

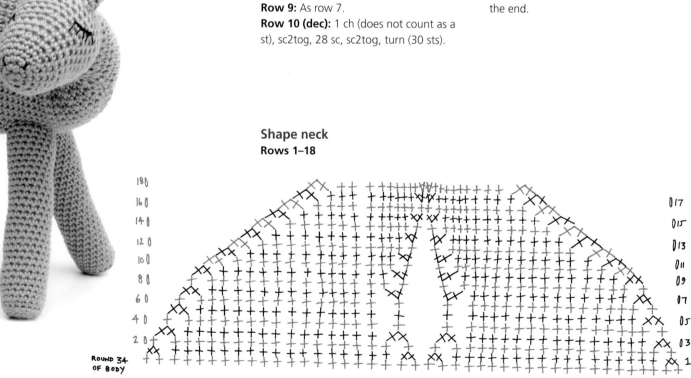

Front legs (make 2)

Starting at the hoof, with C/2–D/3 hook and A, wind yarn around finger a couple of times to form a ring, insert the hook into the ring, catch the yarn and draw it back through the ring.

Round 1: 1 ch (does not count as a st), work 6 sc into ring (6 sts).

Round 2 (inc): (2 sc in next sc) 6 times (12 sts). Pull on short end of yarn to close ring.

Round 3 (inc): (2 sc in next sc, 1 sc) 6 times (18 sts).

Round 4: 1 sc in back loop only of each sc. This will help create a flat base.

Rounds 5–32: Work 1 sc in each sc. Sl st to next st and fasten off.

Front legs

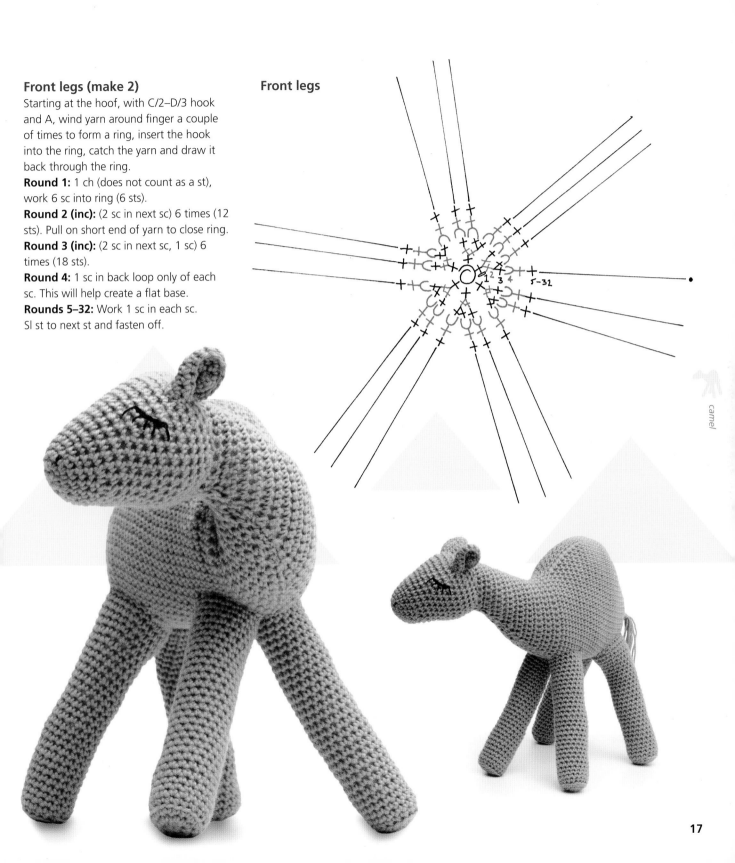

camel

17

Hind legs (make 2)

Starting at the hoof, with C/2–D/3 hook and A, wind yarn around finger a couple of times to form a ring, insert the hook into the ring, catch the yarn and draw it back through the ring.

Work rounds 1–26 as for front legs.

Round 27 (inc): 2 sc in next sc, 1 sc in next 16 sc, 2 sc in next sc (20 sts).

Round 28: Work 1 sc in each sc.

Round 29 (inc): 2 sc in next sc, 1 sc in next 18 sc, 2 sc in next sc (22 sts).

Round 30: Work 1 sc in each sc.

Round 31 (inc): 2 sc in next sc, 1 sc in next 20 sc, 2 sc in next sc (24 sts).

Round 32: Work 1 sc in each sc.
Sl st to next st and fasten off.

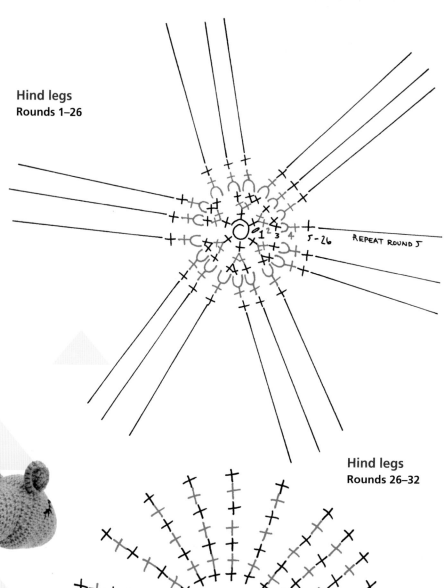

Hind legs
Rounds 1–26

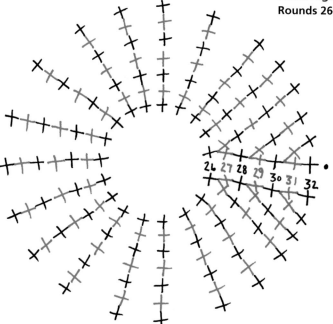

Hind legs
Rounds 26–32

Inner ears (make 2)

With C/2–D/3 hook and A, make 7 ch.

Row 1: 1 sc in second ch from hook, 1 sc in next 4 ch, 3 sc in next ch, 1 sc into each of reverse side of ch, turn (13 sts).

Row 2 (inc) (RS): 1 ch (does not count as a st), 1 sc in next 6 sc, 3sc in next sc, 1 sc in next 6 sc, turn (15 sts).

Fasten off.

Outer ears (make 2)

With C/2–D/3 hook and A, make 7 ch. Work rows 1–2 as for inner ears. Do not fasten off.

Join ear pieces

Place the wrong sides of the ear pieces together with the inner piece facing you. Using C/2–D/3 hook and yarn A, make 1 ch, join the inner and outer ear pieces by working 1 sc in each sc of both ear pieces at the same time, inserting the hook under both loops of each stitch. Fasten off, leaving a long length of yarn. Weave in the short ends.

Ears

JOIN EAR PIECES

camel

DID YOU KNOW?

Camels can kick in all four directions with each of their legs. But not all at the same time!

Tail

With C/2–D/3 hook and A, make 8 ch.
1 sc into second ch from hook, 1 sc into
each of the next 6 ch (7 sts).

Next: 1 ch, sl st into both the back loop of
the next sc and the reverse side of the ch
at the same time to join and form a cord.
Fasten off, leaving a long length of yarn.
Weave in the short end.

Tail

JOIN STITCHES OF TAIL TO FORM A CORD

← NEXT

DID YOU KNOW?
Camels can swim, although
they probably don't get to
practice their breaststroke
much in the desert.

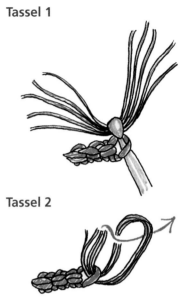

Tassel 1

Tassel 2

Finishing

Body

Stuff the body firmly, filling it to the beginning of the neck shaping. Push the stuffing right into the end of the body and the hump. With the length of yarn left after fastening off, sew the edges of the neck shaping together, matching the rows, then stuff it right to the top of the opening. Stitch the head in position, sewing all around the neck to hold it firmly in place.

Legs

Stuff the legs firmly, filling them right up to the opening and keeping the base of the hooves flat. Stitch the front legs side by side, just before the shaping of the front of the body. Sew the hind legs next to each other with the straight side of the leg facing the back and the shaping going toward the front. Stitch all around each leg to hold them securely in place.

Ears

With the long length of yarn left, sew the lower edges of both ear pieces together to join. Bring the two corners at each side of the lower edge of the ear to the middle and stitch together to shape, with the inner piece on the inside. Sew in place to the head.

Head

Use an air-erasable fabric marker or a tailor's chalk pencil to lightly mark the outline of the eyes and the nostrils. With four strands of black embroidery thread, embroider the curved eye line in chain stitch and embroider five eyelashes in straight stitch. Embroider the nostrils in satin stitch, working just two or three stitches for each one.

Tail

To make the tasseled end of the tail, cut five 8in (20cm) lengths of yarn A and fold the lengths in half to form a loop. Insert the crochet hook into the end of the tail and catch the looped yarn (see Tassel 1). Pull the loop a little way through, remove the hook and then thread the ends back through the loop, pulling them tight (see Tassel 2). Trim the ends and sew the tail in place at the end of the camel.

Apart from the tail, every part of this cute elephant is made entirely in rounds of single crochet. The tusks can be left out if preferred.

Elephant

Information you'll need

Finished size
Approximately 12in (30cm) from head to tail

Materials
Sirdar Snuggly DK (or equivalent DK weight yarn, CYCA 3), 55% nylon, 45% acrylic (179yds/165m per 50g ball)
3 x 50g balls in 427 Baby Gray (A)
Scraps of DK yarn in white (B) and black (C)
B/1–C/2 (UK12:2.5mm) and C/2–D/3 (UK11:3mm) crochet hooks
Toy stuffing
Darning needle
Safety pins

Gauge
22 sts and 24 rounds to 4in (10cm) over single crochet using C/2–D/3 hook

Key

⟋ Chain (ch)

• Slip stitch (sl st)

+ Single crochet (sc)

⤬ 2 sc in same st

╳ sc2tog

⋔ Single crochet into back loop only

⟙ Slip stitch into back loop of single crochet and chain at same time to join

How to make Elephant

Each piece is worked in rounds. All the shaping is done by increasing and decreasing stitches. The head, tusks, body, and legs are stuffed and then stitched together. The ears are flattened and the open edge joined by working a single crochet into both stitches from each side at the same time. Alternatively, they can be sewn together by hand. The corner of each ear is turned and stitched down to shape before sewing to the head. The front and back legs are all made to the same pattern. The eyes are crocheted discs, while the tail is made from a crocheted cord with a tassel attached at the end.

Head
Rounds 1–20

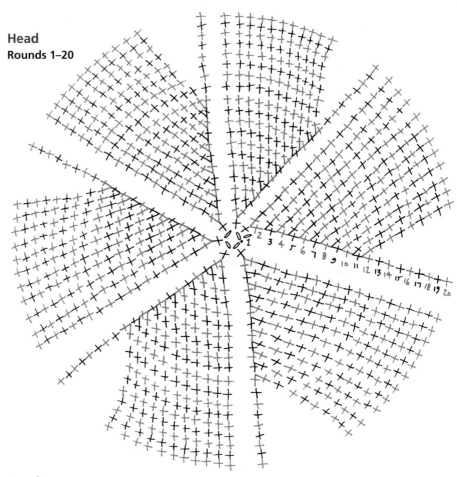

Head

Starting at the top of the head, with C/2–D/3 hook and A, make 4 ch and sl st to first ch to form a ring.

Round 1: 1 ch (does not count as a st), work 6 sc into ring (6 sts).

Round 2 (inc): (2 sc in next sc) 6 times (12 sts).

Round 3 (inc): (2 sc in next sc, 1 sc) 6 times (18 sts).

Round 4 (inc): (2 sc in next sc, 2 sc) 6 times (24 sts).

Round 5 (inc): (2 sc in next sc, 3 sc) 6 times (30 sts).

Round 6 (inc): (2 sc in next sc, 4 sc) 6 times (36 sts).

Round 7 (inc): (2 sc in next sc, 5 sc) 6 times (42 sts).

Round 8 (inc): (2 sc in next sc, 6 sc) 6 times (48 sts).

Round 9 (inc): (2 sc in next sc, 7 sc) 6 times (54 sts).

Round 10 (inc): (2 sc in next sc, 8 sc) 6 times (60 sts).

Round 11 (inc): (2 sc in next sc, 9 sc) 6 times (66 sts).

Round 12 (inc): (2 sc in next sc, 10 sc) 6 times (72 sts).

Rounds 13–20: Work 1 sc in each sc.

Round 21 (dec): (Sc2tog, 10 sc) 6 times (66 sts).

Rounds 22–24: Work 1 sc in each sc.
Round 25 (dec): (Sc2tog, 9 sc) 6 times (60 sts).
Round 26: Work 1 sc in each sc.
Round 27 (dec): (Sc2tog, 8 sc) 6 times (54 sts).
Round 28: Work 1 sc in each sc.
Round 29 (dec): (Sc2tog, 7 sc) 6 times (48 sts).
Round 30: Work 1 sc in each sc.
Round 31 (dec): (Sc2tog, 6 sc) 6 times (42 sts).
Round 32: Work 1 sc in each sc.
Round 33 (dec): (Sc2tog, 5 sc) 6 times (36 sts).
Round 34: Work 1 sc in each sc.
Round 35 (dec): (Sc2tog, 4 sc) 6 times (30 sts).
Rounds 36–40: Work 1 sc in each sc. Do not fasten off. Stuff the head, filling it to just a few rounds below the opening.
Round 41 (dec): (Sc2tog, 3 sc) 6 times (24 sts).
Rounds 42–46: Work 1 sc in each sc.
Round 47 (dec): (Sc2tog, 2 sc) 6 times (18 sts).
Round 48: Work 1 sc in each sc. Add more stuffing before continuing.
Shape trunk
Rounds 49–54: Sc2tog, 6 sc, (2sc in next sc) twice, 6 sc, sc2tog. This puts a curve in the trunk.
Shape end
Round 55: Work 1 sc into the back loop only of each sc.
Round 56 (dec): (Sc2tog, 1 sc) 6 times (12 sts).
Sl st to next st and fasten off, leaving a long length of yarn. Stuff the rest of the trunk, filling it right to the end. Thread the length of yarn left after fastening off onto a needle and weave it in and out of the last round of stitches, draw up, closing the opening, and stitch neatly to secure.

Head
Rounds 20–30

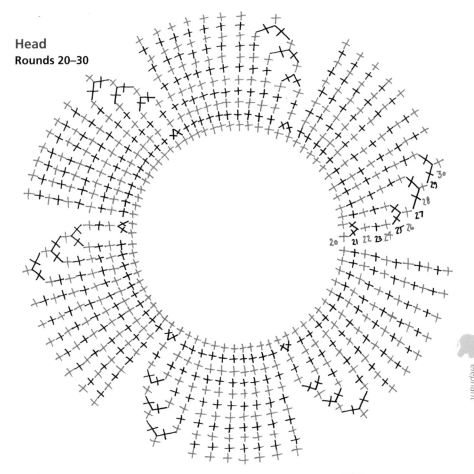

20 21 22 23 24 25 26 27 28 29 30

elephant

JUMBO SNACKS
Elephants can spend up to 16 hours a day collecting leaves, twigs, bamboo, and roots. They don't have time to snack between meals.

25

Head
Rounds 30–46

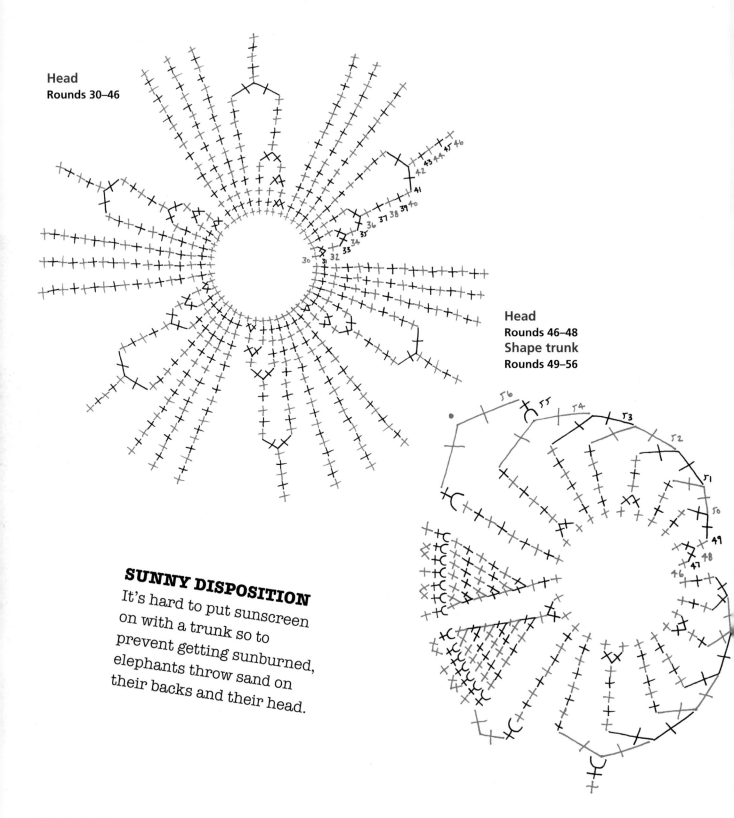

Head
Rounds 46–48
Shape trunk
Rounds 49–56

SUNNY DISPOSITION
It's hard to put sunscreen on with a trunk so to prevent getting sunburned, elephants throw sand on their backs and their head.

Body
Rounds 1–42

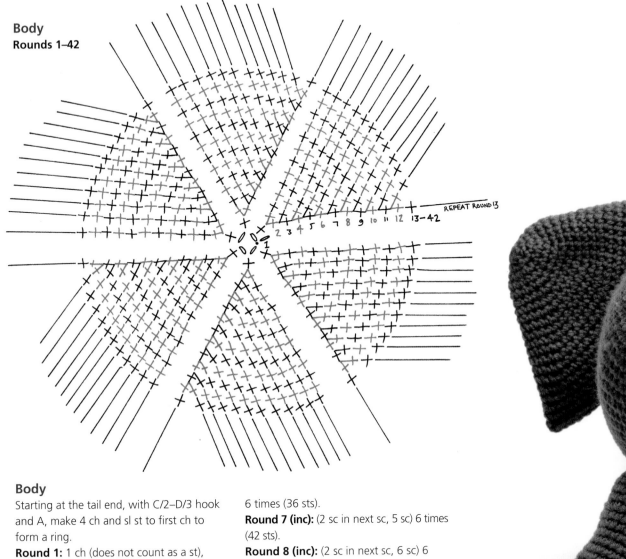

2 3 4 5 6 7 8 9 10 11 12 13-42   REPEAT ROUND 13

Body

Starting at the tail end, with C/2–D/3 hook and A, make 4 ch and sl st to first ch to form a ring.

Round 1: 1 ch (does not count as a st), work 6 sc into ring (6 sts).

Round 2 (inc): (2 sc in next sc) 6 times (12 sts).

Round 3 (inc): (2 sc in next sc, 1 sc) 6 times (18 sts).

Round 4 (inc): (2 sc in next sc, 2 sc) 6 times (24 sts).

Round 5 (inc): (2 sc in next sc, 3 sc) 6 times (30 sts).

Round 6 (inc): (2 sc in next sc, 4 sc) 6 times (36 sts).

Round 7 (inc): (2 sc in next sc, 5 sc) 6 times (42 sts).

Round 8 (inc): (2 sc in next sc, 6 sc) 6 times (48 sts).

Round 9 (inc): (2 sc in next sc, 7 sc) 6 times (54 sts).

Round 10 (inc): (2 sc in next sc, 8 sc) 6 times (60 sts).

Round 11 (inc): (2 sc in next sc, 9 sc) 6 times (66 sts).

Round 12 (inc): (2 sc in next sc, 10 sc) 6 times (72 sts).

Rounds 13–42: Work 1 sc in each sc.

27

Shape front

Round 43 (dec): (Sc2tog, 6 sc) 9 times (63 sts).
Round 44 (dec): (Sc2tog, 5 sc) 9 times (54 sts).
Round 45 (dec): (Sc2tog, 4 sc) 9 times (45 sts).
Round 46 (dec): (Sc2tog, 3 sc) 9 times (36 sts).

Neck

Rounds 47–48: Work 1 sc in each sc.
Sl st to next st and fasten off, leaving a long length of yarn.

Legs (make 4)

Starting at the base, with C/2–D/3 hook and A, make 4 ch and sl st to first ch to form a ring.
Round 1: 1 ch (does not count as a st), work 6 sc into ring (6 sts).
Round 2 (inc): (2 sc in next sc) 6 times (12 sts).

Round 3 (inc): (2 sc in next sc, 1 sc) 6 times (18 sts).
Round 4 (inc): (2 sc in next sc, 2 sc) 6 times (24 sts).
Round 5 (inc): (2 sc in next sc, 3 sc) 6 times (30 sts).
Round 6 (inc): (2 sc in next sc, 4 sc) 6 times (36 sts).
Round 7: Work 1 sc into the back loop only of each sc. This will help create a flat base.
Rounds 8–28: Work 1 sc in each sc.
Sl st to next st and fasten off.

Body Round 42
Shape front Rounds 43–46
Neck Rounds 47–48

Legs

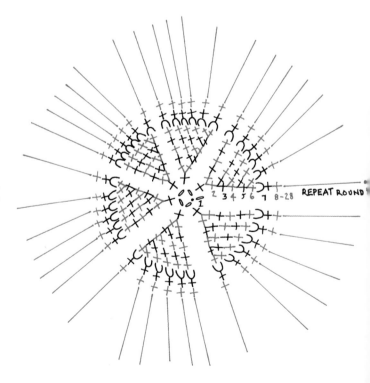

Ears (make 2)

Starting at the base, with C/2–D/3 hook and A, make 4 ch and sl st to first ch to form a ring.

Round 1: 1 ch (does not count as a st), work 6 sc into ring (6 sts).

Round 2 (inc): (2 sc in next sc) 6 times (12 sts).

Round 3 (inc): (2 sc in next sc, 1 sc) 6 times (18 sts).

Round 4 (inc): (2 sc in next sc, 2 sc) 6 times (24 sts).

Round 5: Work 1 sc in each sc.

Round 6 (inc): (2 sc in next sc, 3 sc) 6 times (30 sts).

Round 7 (inc): (2 sc in next sc, 4 sc) 6 times (36 sts).

Round 8: Work 1 sc in each sc.

Round 9 (inc): (2 sc in next sc, 5 sc) 6 times (42 sts).

Round 10 (inc): (2 sc in next sc, 6 sc) 6 times (48 sts).

Round 11: Work 1 sc in each sc.

Round 12 (inc): (2 sc in next sc, 7 sc) 6 times (54 sts).

Round 13 (inc): (2 sc in next sc, 8 sc) 6 times (60 sts).

Round 14: Work 1 sc in each sc.

Round 15 (inc): (2 sc in next sc, 9 sc) 6 times (66 sts).

Round 16 (inc): (2 sc in next sc, 10 sc) 6 times (72 sts).

Round 17: Work 1 sc in each sc.

Round 18 (inc): (2 sc in next sc, 11 sc) 6 times (78 sts).

Round 19 (inc): (2 sc in next sc, 12 sc) 6 times (84 sts).

Round 20: Work 1 sc in each sc.

Join edges

Flatten the shape, matching the stitches on both sides. With C/2–D/3 hook and A, make 1 ch (does not count as a st), insert the hook under both loops of the first stitch and under both loops of the stitch on the other side, work 1 sc to join the two stitches. Continue down the ear, working 1 sc into each of the 42 sc on both sides at the same time to join. Fasten off.

DID YOU KNOW?

Elephants don't like peanuts. They probably prefer potato chips.

elephant

Ears
Rounds 1–20

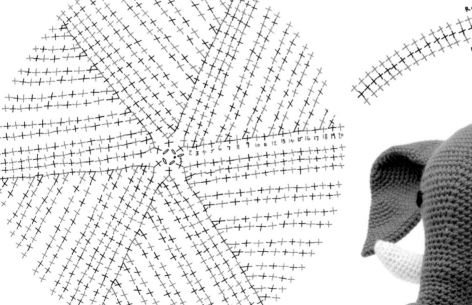

Ear

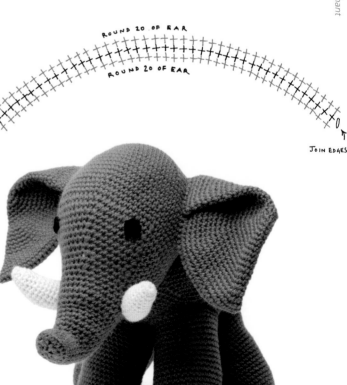

Tusks (make 2)

Starting at the tip of the tusk, with B/1–C/2 hook and B, make 4 ch and sl st to first ch to form a ring.

Round 1: 1 ch (does not count as a st), work 6 sc into ring (6 sts).

Round 2: Work 1 sc in each sc. This round tends to turn inside out, but will get easier as you increase the stitches on the next round. Alternatively, it can be pushed right side out with the end of the hook.

Round 3 (inc): (2 sc in next sc) 6 times (12 sts).

Rounds 4–6: Work 1 sc in each sc.

Round 7 (inc): (2 sc in next sc, 1 sc) 6 times (18 sts).

Round 8: Work 1 sc in each sc.

Shape tusk

Round 9: Sc2tog, 6 sc, (2 sc in next sc) twice, 6 sc, sc2tog.

Round 10: Work 1 sc in each sc.

Rounds 11–14: Rep rounds 9–10 twice more.

Rounds 15–17: As round 9.

Sl st to next st and fasten off, leaving a long length of yarn.

Tusk

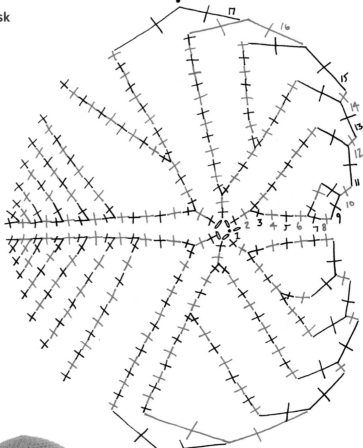

EAR EAR!

You can tell African and Asian elephants apart by the size of their ears—African ones have much larger ears.

elephant

Eyes

Tail

± ± ± ± ± ± ± ± ± ± ± ± ± ± ± 0

○ ○ ○ ○ ○ ○ ○ ○ ○ ○ ○ ○ ○ ○ ○
+ + + + + + + + + + + + + + + 0 ← NEXT

JOIN STITCHES TO FORM A CORD

Eyes (make 2)

With B/1–C/2 hook and C, make 4 ch and sl st to first ch to form a ring.
Next: 1 ch (does not count as a st), work 6 sc into ring (6 sts).
Sl st to next st and fasten off, leaving a length of yarn.

Tail

With C/2–D/3 hook and A, make 16 ch.
1 sc into second ch from hook, 1 sc into each of the next 14 ch (15 sts).
Next: 1 ch, sl st into both the back loop of the next sc and the reverse side of the ch at the same time to join and form a cord.
Fasten off, leaving a long length of yarn.
Weave in the short end.

Finishing

Body

Stuff the body, filling it to the last round of stitches. Use safety pins to hold the head in position. Using the length of yarn left after fastening off, sew the head in place to the neck, stitching all the way around and adding a little more stuffing if necessary to keep it firm.

Legs

Stuff the legs, filling them right up to the opening and keeping the base flat. Stitch the front legs side by side just before the front shaping and sew the back legs right behind them, grouping them close together so they touch. Stitch all around each leg to hold them securely in place.

Ears

Turn 1½in (4cm) over on one corner of the first ear and stitch it down along the long curved edge (see Ear). Repeat with the other ear, folding it at the opposite corner so they mirror each other. Sew the ears in place with the folded edge at the top, stitching around 2¾in (7cm) down and leaving the rest free.

Tusks

Stuff the tusks then flatten the top and sew the nine stitches from each side together to form a straight seam. Sew the tusks to the top of the trunk along the straight seam and a little way down the side of each tusk and into the trunk to keep it from swinging out. Sew the eyes neatly in place.

Tail

To make the tasseled end of the tail, cut four 4in (10cm) lengths of yarn A and fold the lengths in half to form a loop. Insert the crochet hook into the end of the tail and catch the looped yarn (see Tassel 1). Pull the loop a little way through, remove the hook and then thread the ends back through the loop, pulling them tight (see Tassel 2). Trim the ends and sew the tail in place at the end of the body, using the long length of yarn left after fastening off.

DID YOU KNOW?
Elephants' ears are made up of a complex network of blood vessels, which help to regulate the elephant's temperature.

elephant

Ear

Tassel 1

Tassel 2

The body and head of this cuddly polar bear are worked in one whole piece, with the crocheted round nose and simple embroidered eyes adding a serene expression to this not-so-fierce-looking animal.

Polar bear

Information you'll need

Finished size

Approximately 9½in (24cm) from nose to tail

Materials

Bergère de France Lima (or equivalent Sport weight yarn, CYCA 2), 80% wool, 20% alpaca (120yds/110m per 50g ball)
2 x 50g balls in 20441 Polaire (A)
Scrap of DK yarn in black
C/2–D/3 (UK11:3mm) crochet hook
Toy stuffing
Darning needle
Air-erasable fabric marker or tailor's chalk pencil

Gauge

26 sts and 28 rounds to 4in (10cm) over single crochet using C/2–D/3 hook

Key

⌒ Chain (ch)

• Slip stitch (sl st)

+ Single crochet (sc)

✕✕ 2sc in next st

✕✕ sc2tog

⋔ Single crochet into back loop only

How to make Polar bear

Each piece in this project is worked in continuous rounds of single crochet. All of the shaping is formed by increasing and decreasing stitches. The back legs are crocheted so they slope, whereas the front legs are worked straight, but will slope in the same direction when stitched to the shaping at the front of the body. The ears are crocheted spheres that are flattened and then stitched to create the shaping. The tail is worked in rounds and flattened before attaching to the body. The bear is finished with a crocheted nose and embroidered eyes.

Body
Rounds 1–31

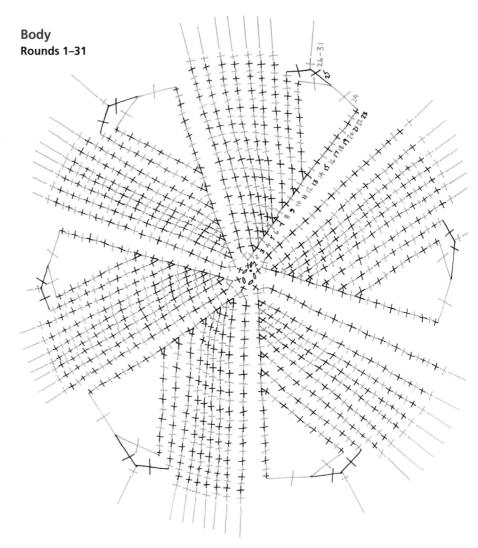

Body

Starting at the tail end, with C/2–D/3 hook and A, make 4 ch and join with a sl st to form a ring.

Round 1: 1 ch (does not count as a st), work 6 sc into ring (6 sts).

Round 2 (inc): (2 sc in next sc) 6 times (12 sts).

Round 3 (inc): (2 sc in next sc, 1 sc) 6 times (18 sts).

Round 4 (inc): (2 sc in next sc, 2 sc) 6 times (24 sts).

Round 5 (inc): (2 sc in next sc, 3 sc) 6 times (30 sts).

Round 6 (inc): (2 sc in next sc, 4 sc) 6 times (36 sts).

Round 7 (inc): (2 sc in next sc, 5 sc) 6 times (42 sts).

Round 8: Work 1 sc in each sc.

Round 9 (inc): (2 sc in next sc, 6 sc) 6 times (48 sts).

Round 10: Work 1 sc in each sc.
Round 11 (inc): (2 sc in next sc, 7 sc) 6 times (54 sts).
Round 12: Work 1 sc in each sc.
Round 13 (inc): (2 sc in next sc, 8 sc) 6 times (60 sts).
Rounds 14–23: Work 1 sc in each sc.
Round 24 (dec): (Sc2tog, 8 sc) 6 times (54 sts).
Round 25 (dec): (Sc2tog, 7 sc) 6 times (48 sts).
Rounds 26–31: Work 1 sc in each sc.

DID YOU KNOW?

Polar bears wag their heads from side to side when they want to play.

Body Round 31
Shape front
Rounds 32–42

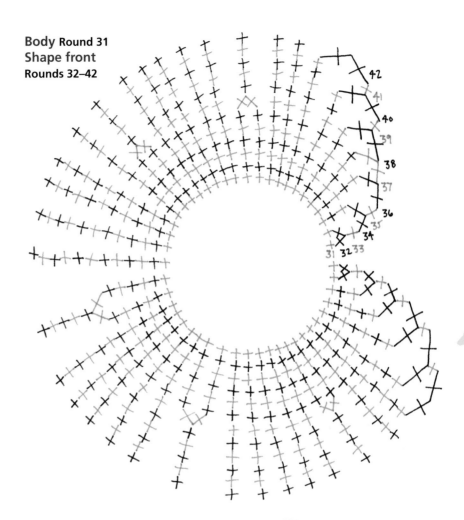

polar bear

Shape front

Round 32 (dec): Sc2tog, 1 sc in each of the next 44 sc, sc2tog (46 sts).
Round 33: Work 1 sc in each sc.
Round 34 (dec): Sc2tog, 1 sc in each of the next 42 sc, sc2tog (44 sts).
Round 35: Work 1 sc in each sc.
Round 36 (dec): Sc2tog, 1 sc in each of the next 40 sc, sc2tog (42 sts).
Round 37 (dec): (Sc2tog, 5 sc) 6 times (36 sts).
Round 38 (dec): Sc2tog, 1 sc in each of the next 32 sc, sc2tog (34 sts).
Round 39: Work 1 sc in each sc.
Round 40 (dec): Sc2tog, 1 sc in each of the next 30 sc, sc2tog (32 sts).
Round 41: Work 1 sc in each sc.
Round 42 (dec): Sc2tog, 1 sc in each of the next 28 sc, sc2tog (30 sts).

37

Head

Rounds 43–50: Work 1 sc in each sc. Do not fasten off. Stuff the body before continuing, filling it to just a few rounds below the previous round.

Shape forehead

Round 51 (dec): With C/2–D/3 hook and A still attached, work 1 sc in next 13 sc, (sc2tog) twice, 1 sc in next 13 sc (28 sts).
Round 52: Work 1 sc in each sc.
Round 53 (dec): Work 1 sc in next 12 sc, (sc2tog) twice, 1 sc in next 12 sc (26 sts).
Round 54: Work 1 sc in each sc.
Round 55 (dec): Work 1 sc in next 11 sc, (sc2tog) twice, 1 sc in next 11 sc (24 sts).
Round 56: Work 1 sc in each sc.
Round 57 (dec): Work 1 sc in next 10 sc, (sc2tog) twice, 1 sc in next 10 sc (22 sts).
Round 58: Work 1 sc in each sc.
Round 59 (dec): Work 1 sc in next 9 sc, (sc2tog) twice, 1 sc in next 9 sc (20 sts).
Round 60 (dec): (Sc2tog, 3 sc) 4 times (16 sts).
Sl st to the next st and fasten off, leaving a long length of yarn at the end.
Weave the yarn through the last round of stitches of the head and finish filling it with the stuffing before drawing up the yarn to close the opening and stitching together to secure.

Body

Round 42
Head
Rounds 43–50
Shape forehead
Rounds 51–60

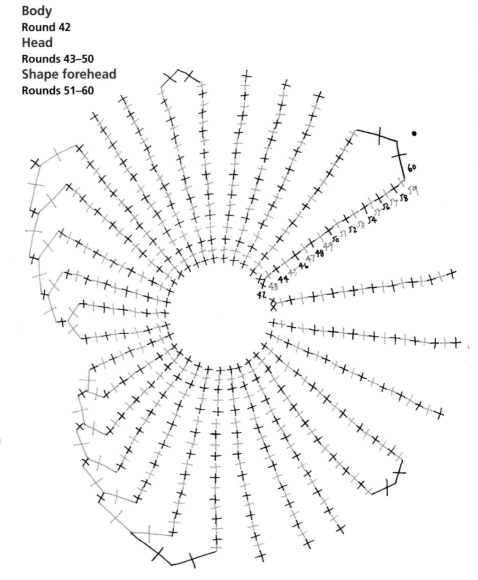

DID YOU KNOW?

Polar bears' ears are small and round and their tails are short and compact. This helps them to conserve heat.

Front legs (make 2)

Starting at the base of the paw, with C/2–D/3 hook and A, make 4 ch and join with a sl st to form a ring.

Round 1: 1 ch (does not count as a st), work 5 sc into ring (5 sts).

Round 2 (inc): (2 sc in next sc) 5 times. (10 sts).

Round 3 (inc): (2 sc in next sc, 1 sc) 5 times (15 sts).

Round 4 (inc): (2 sc in next sc, 2 sc) 5 times (20 sts).

Round 5: 1 sc in back loop only of each sc. This will help create a flat base.

Rounds 6–16: Work 1 sc in each sc. Sl st to next st and fasten off.

Hind legs (make 2)

Starting at the base of the paw, with C/2–D/3 hook and A, make 4 ch and join with a sl st to form a ring.

Round 1: 1 ch (does not count as a st), work 6 sc into ring (6 sts).

Round 2 (inc): (2 sc in next sc) 6 times (12 sts).

Round 3 (inc): (2 sc in next sc, 1 sc) 6 times (18 sts).

Round 4 (inc): (2 sc in next sc, 2 sc) 6 times (24 sts).

Round 5: 1 sc in back loop only of each sc. This will help create a flat base.

Round 6: Work 1 sc in each sc.

Round 7: Sc2tog, 1 sc in next 9 sc, (2 sc

in next sc) twice, 1 sc in next 9 sc, sc2tog.

Round 8: Work 1 sc in each sc.

Rounds 9–16: Rep rounds 6–7 4 times. Sl st to next st and fasten off.

Front legs

Hind legs

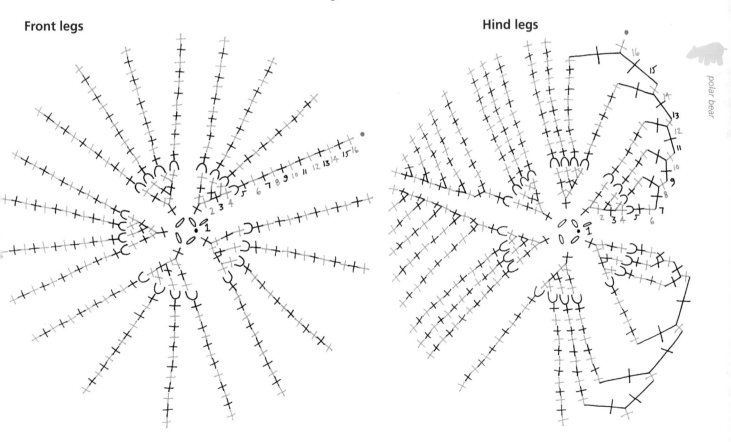

polar bear

Ears

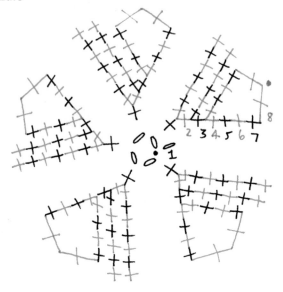

Nose

Tail

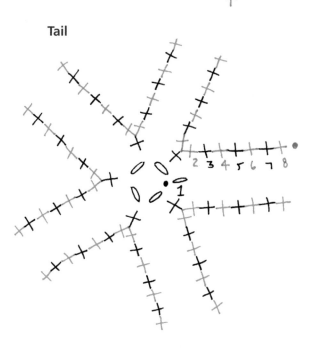

Ears (make 2)

Starting at the top of the ear, with C/2–D/3 hook and A, make 4 ch and join with a sl st to form a ring.

Round 1: 1 ch (does not count as a st), work 5 sc into ring (5 sts).

Round 2 (inc): (2 sc in next sc) 5 times (10 sts).

Round 3 (inc): (2 sc in next sc, 1 sc) 5 times (15 sts).

Round 4 (inc): (2 sc in next sc, 2 sc) 5 times (20 sts).

Rounds 5–7: Work 1 sc in each sc.

Round 8 (dec): (Sc2tog, 2 sc) 5 times (15 sts).Sl st to next st and fasten off, leaving a long length of yarn.

Tail

With C/2–D/3 hook and A, make 4 ch and join with a sl st to form a ring.

Round 1: 1 ch (does not count as a st), 5 sc into the ring (5 sts).

Round 2 (inc): (2 sc in next sc) 5 times (10 sts).

Rounds 3–8: Work 1 sc in each sc. Sl st to next st and fasten off, leaving a long length of yarn.

Nose

With C/2–D/3 hook and black DK yarn, make 4 ch and join with a sl st to form a ring.

Next: 1 ch (does not count as a st), work 6 sc into ring (6 sts).

Sl st to next st and fasten off, leaving a long length of yarn.

ICE AND CLEAN

Polar bears like to keep clean, so after a snack they'll usually wash by taking a swim or rolling in the snow.

Finishing

Body and legs
Stuff the legs, filling them right up to the opening and keeping the base flat. Stitch the front legs to the body side by side, just over the first few rounds of the front shaping, so they naturally slope with the contour of the body. Sew the hind legs in place with the slope in the legs facing toward the rear end. Stitch all around each leg to hold them securely in place.

Ears
Flatten each ear and, with the long length of yarn left, sew each side together to join. Bring the two corners at the lower edge of the ear to the middle and stitch them together to form a bowl shape. Run a gathering stitch around the lower edge of the ear, draw up and secure with a few stitches before sewing in place to each side of the head.

Tail
Flatten the tail and sew the 5 sc on each side together to join using the long length of yarn left after fastening off. Stitch in place at the end of the polar bear.

Eyes
Use the length of yarn left after fastening off the nose to sew it neatly into position at the end of the face. Then mark the position of the eyes on the bear with an air-erasable fabric marker or a tailor's chalk pencil. Use the black DK yarn to embroider the eyes in stem stitch.

The yarn used for this project is quite thick and, with the smaller hook, creates a firm, dense fabric. An E/4 hook can be used instead, although this will affect the gauge and the finished size of the deer.

Deer

Information you'll need

Finished size

Approximately 9in (23cm) tall (not including the ears) and around 5in (12.5cm) from the front to the back of the body

Materials

Rowan Handknit Cotton (or equivalent Worsted weight yarn, CYCA 4), 100% cotton (93yds/85m per 50g ball)
2 x 50g balls in 215 Rosso (A)
1 x 50g ball in 251 Ecru (B)
Oddment of DK yarn in black (C)
C/2–D/3 (UK11:3mm) crochet hook
Toy stuffing
Darning needle
Sewing needle
Embroidery needle
Stranded embroidery thread in black
Black sewing thread
2 x black buttons around ⅜in (1cm) in diameter

Gauge

20 sts and 22 rounds to 4in (10cm) over single crochet using C/2–D/3 hook

deer

DID YOU KNOW?
Deer take their first steps within just half an hour of being born.

Key

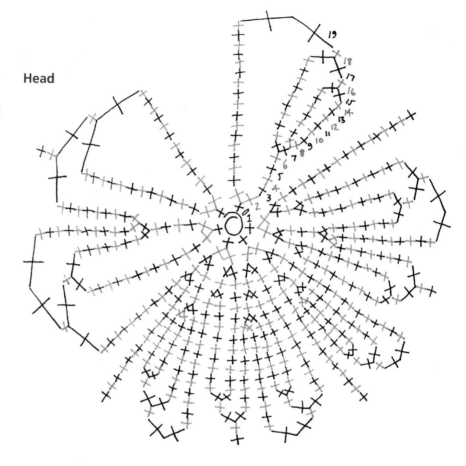

Head

⟳ Wind yarn around finger to form a ring

• Slip stitch (sl st)

∕ Chain (ch)

+ Single crochet (sc)

⤬⤬ 2 sc in same st

⤬⤬ sc2tog

⤬⥮⤬ 3 sc in same st

⑂ Single crochet into back loop only

⑃ Single crochet into back loops of both stitches at the same time to join

⊤ Half double crochet (hdc)

⊤ Double crochet (dc)

How to make Deer

The head is worked in continuous rounds with the face shaped by increasing the stitches under the nose. The body is started in rounds and then finished in rows to shape the front. Stitches are picked up around the opening left after finishing the body shaping to form the neck. The legs are all made in continuous rounds, with the hind legs shaped by increasing the stitches at the front and decreasing at the back. The ears and tail are each worked in two pieces in rows; the pieces are then crocheted together. The crocheted eye pieces are worked in rows with the shaping formed by increasing the stitches and working the longer half

double crochet stiches and double crochet stitches into the pattern. The markings are crocheted in rounds and the pieces of the deer are stitched together. Buttons and embroidered eyelashes finish the eyes.

Head
Starting at the nose tip, with C/2–D/3 hook and B, wind yarn around finger a couple of times to form a ring, insert the hook, catch the yarn and draw back through the ring.
Round 1: 1 ch (does not count as a st), work 6 sc into ring (6 sts).
Round 2 (inc): (2 sc in next sc) 6 times (12 sts). Pull on short end of yarn to close ring.
Round 3 (inc): 1 sc in each of next 6 sc, (2 sc in next sc) 6 times (18 sts).
Round 4: Work 1 sc in each sc.
Round 5 (inc): 1 sc in each of next 6 sc, (2

sc in next sc, 1 sc) 6 times (24 sts).
Round 6: Work 1 sc in each sc.
Round 7 (inc): (2 sc in next sc, 3 sc) 6 times (30 sts). Join and continue in yarn A.
Round 8 (inc): (2 sc in next sc, 4 sc) 6 times (36 sts).
Rounds 9–14: Work 1 sc in each sc.
Shape back of head
Round 15 (dec): (Sc2tog, 2 sc) 9 times (27 sts).
Round 16: Work 1 sc in each sc.
Round 17 (dec): (Sc2tog, 1 sc) 9 times (18 sts).
Round 18: Work 1 sc in each sc.
Round 19 (dec): (Sc2tog, 1 sc) 6 times (12 sts). Fasten off, leaving a length of yarn and thread through the last round of stitches. Stuff the head firmly, gather up the opening and stitch to secure.

Body
Rounds 1–19

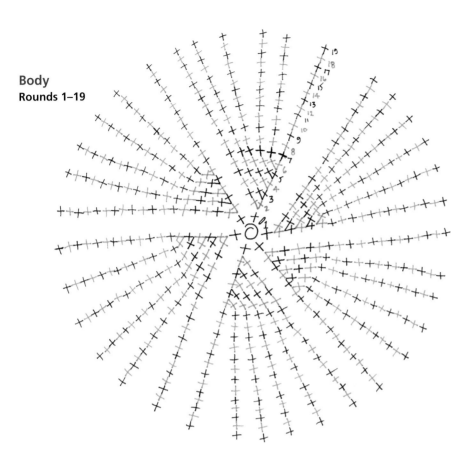

Body

Starting at the tail end of the deer, with C/2–D/3 hook and A, wind yarn around a finger a couple of times to form a ring, insert the hook, catch the yarn and draw back through the ring.

Round 1: 1 ch (does not count as a st), work 6 sc into ring (6 sts).

Round 2 (inc): (2 sc in next sc) 6 times (12 sts). Pull on short end of yarn to close ring.

Round 3 (inc): (2 sc in next sc, 1 sc) 6 times (18 sts).

Round 4 (inc): (2 sc in next sc, 2 sc) 6 times (24 sts).

Round 5 (inc): (2 sc in next sc, 3 sc) 6 times (30 sts).

Round 6 (inc): (2 sc in next sc, 4 sc) 6 times (36 sts).

Rounds 7–19: Work 1 sc in each sc.

Shape front

The following is worked in rows:

Row 1 (RS) (dec): Work 1 sc in next 13 sc, (sc2tog) twice, 1 sc in next 13 sc, turn.

Row 2: 1 ch (does not count as a st), 1 sc in next 28 sc, turn.

Row 3 (dec): 1 ch (does not count as a st), 1 sc in next 12 sc, (sc2tog) twice, 1 sc in next 12 sc, turn.

Row 4: 1 ch (does not count as a st), 1 sc in each 26 sc, turn.

Row 5 (dec): 1 ch (does not count as a st), 1 sc in next 11 sc, (sc2tog) twice, 1 sc in next 11 sc, turn.

Row 6: 1 ch (does not count as a st), 1 sc in each 24 sc, turn.

Row 7 (dec): 1 ch (does not count as a st), 1 sc in next 10 sc, (sc2tog) twice, 1 sc in next 10 sc, turn.

Shape front of body
Rows 1–7

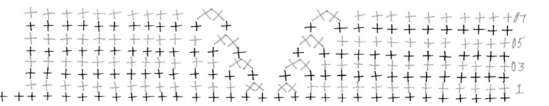

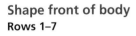

45

Join center front

Row 8: With both sides together and right side facing, 1 ch, then work 1 sc into the back loops only of each of the 11 sc from both sides at the same time to join. This will leave an opening at the top of the body for the neck shaping. Fasten off.

Shape neck

With right side facing, with C/2–D/3 hook and A, rejoin yarn to the center front of the opening at the top of the body.

Round 1: Work 1 sc in the stitches at the end of each of the 7 rows of the front shaping, 1 sc in each of the next 6 sc of the back, work 1 sc in the stitches at the opposite end of the 7 rows of the front shaping (20 sts).

Round 2 (dec): (Sc2tog, 2 sc) 5 times (15 sts).

Rounds 3–6: Work 1 sc in each sc. Sl st to next st and fasten off.

Front legs (make 2)

Starting at the hoof, with C/2–D/3 hook and C, wind yarn around finger a couple of times to form a ring, insert the hook into the ring, catch the yarn and draw it back through the ring.

Round 1: 1 ch (does not count as a st), work 6 sc into ring (6 sts).

Round 2 (inc): (2 sc in next sc) 6 times (12 sts). Pull on short end of yarn to close ring.

Round 3: 1 sc in back loop only of each sc. This will help create a flat base.

Rounds 4–6: Work 1 sc in each sc. Join and continue in A.

Rounds 7–22: Work 1 sc in each sc. Sl st to next st and fasten off.

Joint center front

Shape neck

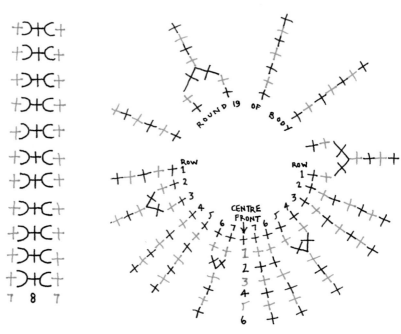

Front legs

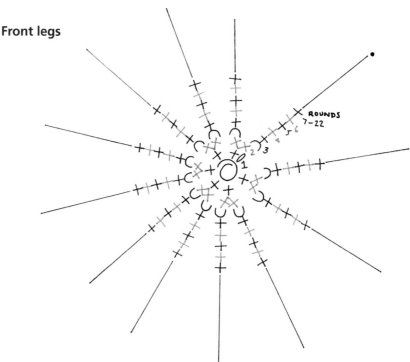

Hind legs (make 2)

Starting at the hoof, with C/2–D/3 hook and C, wind yarn around finger a couple of times to form a ring, insert the hook into the ring, catch the yarn and draw it back through the ring.

Work rounds 1–18 as for front legs.

Round 19 (inc): 2 sc in next sc, 1 sc in next 10 sc, 2 sc in next sc (14 sts).

Round 20 (inc): 2 sc in next sc, 1 sc in next 12 sc, 2 sc in next sc (16 sts).

Round 21 (inc): 2 sc in next sc, 1 sc in next 14 sc, 2 sc in next sc (18 sts).

Shape top of leg

Round 22 (inc): (2 sc in next sc) twice, 1 sc in next 5 sc, (sc2tog) twice, 1 sc in next 5 sc, (2 sc in next sc) twice (20 sts).

Round 23 (inc): (2 sc in next sc) twice, 1 sc in next 6 sc, (sc2tog) twice, 1 sc in next 6 sc, (2 sc in next sc) twice (22 sts).

Round 24 (inc): (2 sc in next sc) twice, 1 sc in next 7 sc, (sc2tog) twice, 1 sc in next 7 sc, (2 sc in next sc) twice (24 sts).
Sl st to next st and fasten off.

Outer ears (make 2)

With C/2–D/3 hook and A, make 9 ch.

Row 1 (RS): 1 sc in second ch from hook, 1 sc in next 6 ch, 3 sc in next ch, 1 sc into each of reverse side of ch, turn (17 sts).

Row 2 (inc): 1 ch (does not count as a st), 1 sc in next 8 sc, 3 sc in next sc, 1 sc in next 8 sc, turn (19 sts).

Row 3 (inc): 1 ch (does not count as a st), 1 sc in next 9 sc, 3 sc in next sc, 1 sc in next 9 sc, turn (21 sts).

Row 4 (inc): 1 ch (does not count as a st), 1 sc in next 10 sc, 3 sc in next sc, 1 sc in next 10 sc, turn (23 sts). Fasten off.

Inner ears (make 2)

With C/2–D/3 hook and B, make 9 ch.
Work rows 1–4 as for outer ears.
Fasten off.

Hind legs

Ears

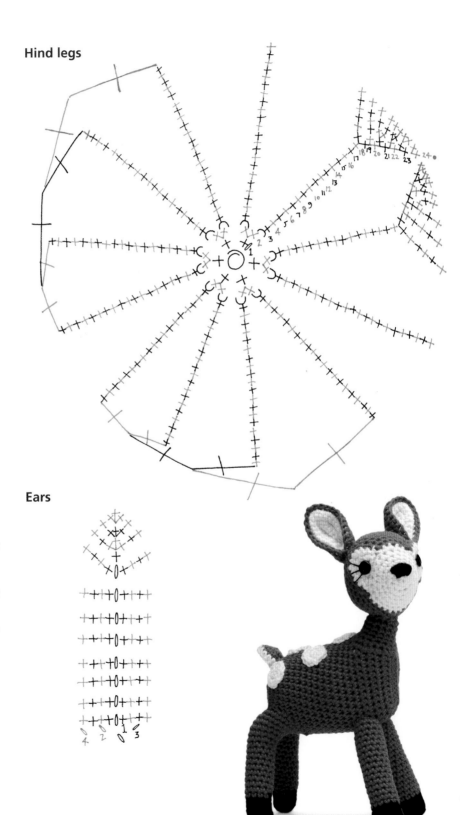

deer

47

Ears

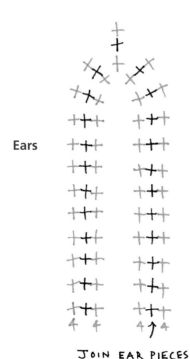

JOIN EAR PIECES

Eyes

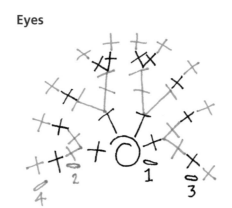

Tail

Join ear pieces
Place the wrong sides of the ear pieces together with the inner piece facing you. Using C/2–D/3 hook and yarn A, join the inner and outer ear pieces by working 1 sc in each sc of both ear pieces at the same time, inserting the hook under both loops of each stitch. Fasten off, leaving a long length. Weave in the short ends.

Eyes (make 2)
With C/2–D/3 hook and B, wind yarn around a finger a few times to form a ring, insert the hook, catch the yarn and draw back through the ring.

Row 1 (WS): 1 ch (does not count as a st), into ring work 1 sc, 2 hdc, 1 sc, turn (4 sts).

Row 2 (RS) (inc): 1 ch (does not count as a st), 2 sc in next sc, (1 hdc, 1 dc) in next hdc, (1 dc, 1 hdc) in next hdc, 2 sc in next sc, turn (8 sts).

Row 3 (inc): 1 ch (does not count as a st), 1 sc in the next 3 sts, (2 sc in next sc) twice, 1 sc in the next 3 sts, turn (10 sts). Pull tight on short end to close ring.

Row 4 (inc): Join A and work 1 sc in each sc.

Fasten off, leaving a long length of yarn at the end in both A and B.

Tail
With C/2–D/3 hook and A, make 5 ch.

Round 1 (RS): 1 sc in second ch from hook, 1 sc in next 2 ch, 3 sc in next ch, 1 sc into each of reverse side of ch (9 sts).

Round 2 (inc): 2 ch, 1 sc in next sc, 2 sc in next sc, 1 sc in next 2 sc, 3 sc in next sc, 1 sc in next 2 sc, 2 sc in next sc, 1 sc in next sc (13 sts).

Sl st into the 2 ch loop and fasten off. To crochet the underside tail piece, use yarn B and C/2–D/3 hook and make 5 ch. Work rounds 1–2 for tail, sl st into the 2 ch loop but do not fasten off at the end.

Tail

JOIN TAIL PIECES

Join tail pieces
Place the wrong sides of the two pieces together with the piece in yarn B facing you. In B, work 1 sc in next 6 sc, 3 sc in next sc, 1 sc in next 6 sc. Sl st into the first sc and fasten off.

Markings

Markings (make 6)
With C/2–D/3 hook and B, wind yarn around finger a couple of times to form a ring, insert the hook into the ring, catch the yarn and draw it back through the ring.
Round 1: 1 ch (does not count as a st), work 6 sc into ring (6 sts).
Round 2 (inc): (2 sc in next sc) 6 times (12 sts), sl st to next st and fasten off. Pull on short end of yarn to close ring.

DID YOU KNOW?
Deer have a great sense of hearing and can turn their ears in any direction without moving their heads. A great party trick!

deer

DID YOU KNOW?
Deer have their eyes on
the sides of their head, so
they can see if predators
are sneaking up on them.

Finishing

Body
Stuff the body firmly, filling it right to the top of the neck opening. Sew the head in place with the sloped shaping in yarn B positioned so it is under the chin, the shorter part being above the nose.

Legs
Stuff the legs firmly right up to the opening and keeping the base of the hooves flat. Stitch the front legs side by side, just behind the front shaping of the body. Sew the hind legs next to each other with the bend in the leg facing toward the back. Stitch all around each leg to hold them securely in place.

Ears
With the long length of yarn left, sew the lower edges of the inner and outer ear pieces together to join. Bring the two corners at each side of the lower edge of the ear to the middle and stitch together to shape, with the inner piece on the inside. Run a gathering stitch around the lower edge of the ear, draw up and secure with a few stitches before sewing in place on the head.

Tail
Stitch the tail in place at the rear of the deer. Sew the markings on the deer's back.

Eyes
Sew the crocheted eye pieces neatly in place using the lengths of yarn left after fastening off, lining the straight edge of the eye up against the last round in yarn B of the face. With three strands of black embroidery thread, work three eyelashes on each eye in straight stitch starting at the center of the lower edge and finishing at the curved outer edge of yarn B. Sew the buttons on for the eyes.

Nose
With yarn C, embroider the nose in satin stitch, working over rounds 2 and 3 of the head at the top front of the face. Weave in all the ends.

deer

DID YOU KNOW?
Fawns are protected by a lack of scent so their enemies cannot smell them.

Worked mainly in rounds of single crochet stitches, this foxy fellow looks very smart in his orange coat, white bib, and black socks. His beady eyes can be replaced with embroidered French knots.

Fox

Information you'll need

Finished size
Approximately 16in (41cm) high (not including the ears)

Materials
Adriafil Regina (or equivalent DK weight yarn, CYCA 3), 100% merino wool (137yds/125m per 50g ball)
2 x 50g balls in 035 Dark Orange (A)
1 x 50g ball in 001 Black (B)
1 x 50g ball in 011 Cream (C)
C/2–D/3 (UK11:3mm) crochet hook
Darning needle
Toy stuffing
Embroidery needle
Stranded embroidery thread in black
Sewing needle
Black sewing thread
2 x black beads around ¼in (0.5cm) in diameter

Gauge
24 sts and 28 rounds to 4in (10cm) over single crochet using C/2–D/3 hook

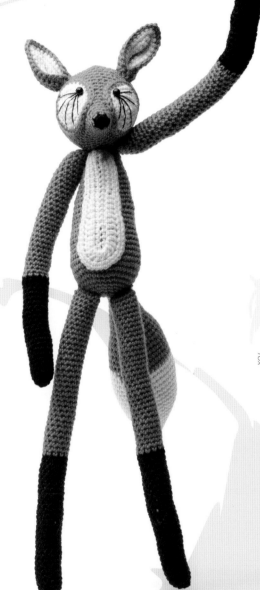

fox

DID YOU KNOW?
Foxes have whiskers on their legs as well as around their faces.

53

Key

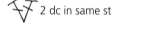 Chain (ch)

• Slip stitch (sl st)

+ Single crochet (sc)

✕✕ 2 sc in same st

✕✕ sc2tog

✕✕✕ 3 sc in same st

T Half double (hdc)

丅 Double (dc)

✕✕✕ 2 dc in same st

Head

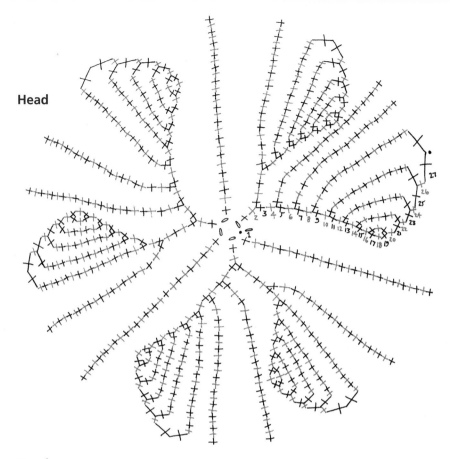

How to make Fox

Single crochet is used for most of Fox except the bib, which incorporates half double and double stitches. Head, body, and eye patches are worked in continuous rounds of single crochet with shaping formed by increasing the stitches. The tail is shaped with extra stitches added on just one side, creating a different curved effect. Legs are straight tubes crocheted in continuous rounds. The ears are made in rows, turning the work instead of continuing around it. The features are embroidered, with beads for eyes.

Head

Starting at the nose, with C/2–D/3 hook and B, make 4 ch and join with a sl st to the first ch to form a ring.
Round 1: 1 ch (does not count as a st), work 6 sc into ring (6 sts).
Join and continue in A.
Round 2: Work 1 sc in each sc.
Round 3 (inc): (2 sc in next sc, 1 sc) 3 times (9 sts).
Round 4: Work 1 sc in each sc.
Round 5 (inc): (2 sc in next sc, 2 sc) 3 times (12 sts).
Round 6: Work 1 sc in each sc.
Round 7 (inc): (2 sc in next sc, 1 sc) 6 times (18 sts).
Round 8: Work 1 sc in each sc.
Round 9 (inc): (2 sc in next sc, 2 sc) 6 times (24 sts).
Round 10: Work 1 sc in each sc.
Round 11 (inc): (2 sc in next sc, 3 sc)

6 times (30 sts).
Round 12: Work 1 sc in each sc.
Round 13 (inc): (2 sc in next sc, 4 sc) 6 times (36 sts).
Round 14: Work 1 sc in each sc.
Round 15 (inc): (2 sc in next sc, 5 sc) 6 times (42 sts).
Round 16: Work 1 sc in each sc.
Round 17 (inc): (2 sc in next sc, 6 sc) 6 times (48 sts).
Round 18: Work 1 sc in each sc.
Round 19 (dec): (Sc2tog, 6 sc) 6 times (42 sts).
Round 20: Work 1 sc in each sc.
Round 21 (dec): (Sc2tog, 5 sc) 6 times (36 sts).
Round 22: Work 1 sc in each sc.
Round 23 (dec): (Sc2tog, 4 sc) 6 times (30 sts).
Round 24: Work 1 sc in each sc.

HIGH ACHIEVERS

Foxes sometimes climb trees and settle on low branches. But they haven't built any tree houses yet as far as anyone knows.

Body

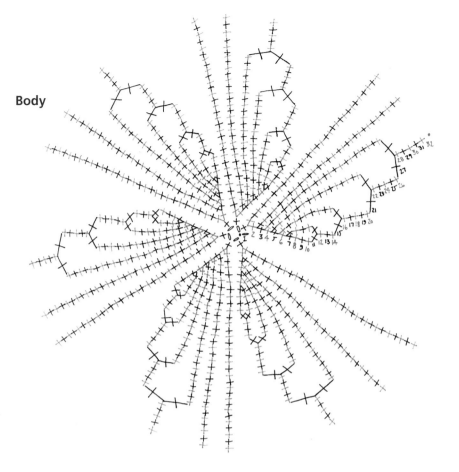

Eye patches

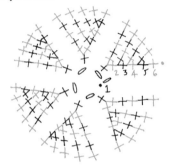

Round 25 (dec): (Sc2tog, 3 sc) 6 times (24 sts).
Round 26: Work 1 sc in each sc.
Round 27 (dec): (Sc2tog, 2 sc) 6 times (18 sts).
Sl st to the next st and fasten off, leaving a long length of yarn at the end.

Eye patches (make 2)

Leaving length of yarn at beginning, with C/2–D/3 hook and C, make 4 ch and join with a sl st to the first ch to form a ring.
Round 1: 1 ch (does not count as a st), work 6 sc into ring (6 sts).
Round 2 (inc): (2 sc in next sc) 6 times (12 sts).
Round 3 (inc): (2 sc in next sc, 1 sc) 6 times(18 sts).
Round 4 (inc): (2 sc in next sc, 2 sc) 6 times (24 sts).

Round 5 (inc): (2 sc in next sc, 3 sc) 6 times (30 sts).
Round 6 (inc): Join A and work 1 sc in each sc.
Sl st to next st and fasten off, leaving a long length of yarn at the end.

Body

With C/2–D/3 hook and B, make 4 ch and join with a sl st to the first ch to form ring.
Round 1: 1 ch (does not count as a st), work 6 sc into ring (6 sts).
Round 2 (inc): (2 sc in next sc) 6 times (12 sts).
Round 3 (inc): (2 sc in next sc, 1 sc) 6 times (18 sts).
Round 4 (inc): (2 sc in next sc, 2 sc) 6 times (24 sts).
Round 5 (inc): (2 sc in next sc, 3 sc) 6 times (30 sts).

Round 6 (inc): (2 sc in next sc, 4 sc) 6 times (36 sts).
Round 7 (inc): (2 sc in next sc, 5 sc) 6 times (42 sts).
Rounds 8–10: Work 1 sc in each sc.
Round 11 (dec): (Sc2tog, 5 sc) 6 times (36 sts).
Rounds 12–14: Work 1 sc in each sc.
Round 15 (dec): (Sc2tog, 4 sc) 6 times (30 sts).
Rounds 16–20: Work 1 sc in each sc.
Round 21 (dec): (Sc2tog, 3 sc) 6 times (24 sts).
Rounds 22–26: Work 1 sc in each sc.
Round 27 (dec): (Sc2tog, 2 sc) 6 times (18 sts).
Rounds 28–32: Work 1 sc in each sc.
Sl st to next st and fasten off, leaving a long length of yarn.

fox

Bib

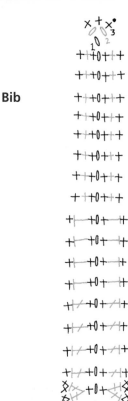

Ears

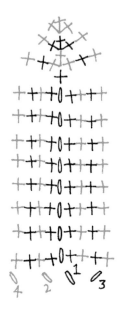

Join ear pieces

Bib

With C/2–D/3 hook and C, make 19 ch.
Round 1: 1 sc into second ch from hook, 1 sc in next 16 ch, 3 sc in end ch, 1 sc in reverse side of each ch to end (37 sts).
Round 2 (inc): 2 ch, 1 sc in next 8 sc, 1 hdc in next 4 sc, 1 dc in next 4 sc, (2 dc in same st) 5 times, 1 dc in next 4 sc, 1 hdc in next 4 sc, 1 sc in next 8 sc (42 sts and one 2 ch sp).
Round 3 (inc): Work 3 sc in the 2 ch space, 1 sc in each of next 8 sc, 1 sc in each of next 4 hdc, 1 sc in each of next 4 dc, (2 sc in next sc) in each of next 10 dc, 1 sc in each of next 4 dc, 1 sc in each of next 4 hdc, 1 sc in next 8 sc (55 sts).
Sl st to next st and fasten off, leaving a long length of yarn.

Inner ears (make 2)

With C/2–D/3 hook and C, make 9 ch.
Row 1 (RS): 1 sc in second ch from hook, 1 sc in next 6 ch, 3 sc in next ch, 1 sc into each of reverse side of ch, turn (17 sts).
Row 2 (inc): 1 ch (does not count as a st), 1 sc in next 8 sc, 3 sc in next sc, 1 sc in next 8 sc, turn (19 sts).
Row 3 (inc): 1 ch (does not count as a st), 1 sc in next 9 sc, 3 sc in next sc, 1 sc in next 9 sc, turn (21 sts).
Row 4 (inc): 1 ch (does not count as a st), 1 sc in next 10 sc, 3 sc in next sc, 1 sc in next 10 sc (23 sts). Fasten off.

Outer ears (make 2)

With C/2–D/3 hook and A, make 9 ch and work as for inner ear.

Join ear pieces

Place the wrong sides of the ear pieces together with the inner piece facing you. Using C/2–D/3 hook and yarn A, join the inner and outer ear pieces by working 1 sc in each of the next 11 sc of both ear pieces at the same time, inserting the hook under both loops of each stitch, 3 sc into the next sc of both pieces at the same time to shape the pointed tip of the ear, 1 sc in each of the next 11 sc of both ear pieces at the same time. Fasten off, leaving a long length. Weave in the short ends.

Legs

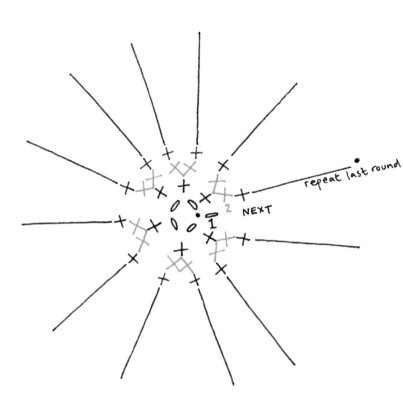

fox

Back legs (make 2)

With C/2–D/3 hook and B, make 4 ch and join with a sl st to form a ring.

Round 1: 1 ch (does not count as a st), work 6 sc into ring (6 sts).

Round 2 (inc): (2 sc in next sc) 6 times (12 sts).

Next: Work 1 sc in each sc until leg measures 4in (10cm).
Join and continue with yarn A.

Next: Work 1 sc in each sc until leg measures 8⅝in (22cm).
Sl st to next st and fasten off.

Front legs (make 2)

With C/2–D/3 hook and B, make 4 ch and join with a sl st to form a ring.

Work rounds 1–2 as for the back legs.

Next: Work 1 sc in each sc until leg measures 3⅛in (8cm).
Join and continue with yarn A.

Next: Work 1 sc in each sc until leg measures 7in (18cm).
Sl st to next st and fasten off.

COME DINE WITH ME

Foxes are easy dinner guests; they eat just about anything, including berries, worms, and spiders.

Tail

With C/2–D/3 hook and C, make 4 ch and join with a sl st to form a ring.

Round 1: 1 ch (does not count as a st), work 6 sc into ring (6 sts).

Round 2 (inc): (2 sc in next sc) 6 times (12 sts).

Round 3: Work 1 sc in each sc.

Shape tail

Round 4 (inc): (2 sc in next sc) 6 times, 1 sc in next 6 sc (18 sts).

Round 5: Work 1 sc in each sc.

Round 6 (inc): (2 sc in next sc, 1 sc) 6 times, 1 sc in next 6 sc (24 sts).

Round 7: Work 1 sc in each sc.

Round 8 (inc): (2 sc in next sc, 2 sc) 6 times, 1 sc in next 6 sc (30 sts).

Round 9: Work 1 sc in each sc.

Round 10 (inc): (2 sc in next sc, 3 sc) 6 times, 1 sc in next 6 sc (36 sts).

Rounds 11–19: Work 1 sc in each sc. Join and continue in A.

Round 20–21: Work 1 sc in each sc.

Round 22 (dec): (Sc2tog, 3 sc) 6 times, 1 sc in next 6 sc (30 sts).

Rounds 23–24: Work 1 sc in each sc.

Round 25 (dec): (Sc2tog, 2 sc) 6 times, 1 sc in next 6 sc (24 sts).

Rounds 26–27: Work 1 sc in each sc.

Round 28 (dec): (Sc2tog, 1 sc) 6 times, 1 sc in next 6 sc (18 sts).

Rounds 29–30: Work 1 sc in each sc.

Round 31 (dec): (Sc2tog) 6 times, 1 sc in next 6 sc (12 sts).

Rounds 32–40: Work 1 sc in each sc. Sl st to next st and fasten off, leaving a long length of yarn.

DID YOU KNOW?

Foxes can reach speeds of 30mph (48km/h).

Tail

Finishing

Head

Using a blunt-ended darning needle, weave the yarn through the last round of stitches of the head, then stuff firmly before drawing up the yarn to close the opening and stitch together to secure.

Eyes

Attach the eye patches to each side of the face, using the long length of A to sew around the outside of the shape and the length of C left to catch down the center of the circular patch with a few stitches. Embroider the eyelashes in straight stitch with three strands of black embroidery thread, then sew on the beads for the eyes. Alternatively, work a French knot for each eye.

Ears

With the long length of yarn left, sew the lower edges of the inner and outer ear pieces together to join them. Bring the two corners at each side of the lower edge of the ear to the middle and stitch together to shape, with the inner piece on the inside. Run a gathering stitch around the lower edge of the ear, draw up and secure with a few stitches before sewing in place on the head.

Body

Stuff the body firmly and use a darning needle to weave the length of yarn left at the end through the last round of stitches. Draw up to gather and sew a few stitches over each other to secure.

Bib

Use the length of yarn left at the end of the bib to sew it to the front of the body with the narrow end at the neck. Stitch the head to the body, sewing all around the neck to join securely and prevent it from flopping about.

Legs

Stuff the front and back legs. Stitch the top end of each leg by squeezing it together and sewing the stitches from each side to form a straight seam. Sew the seam at the top of the front legs in place along the neckline and the back legs to the lower end of the body.

Tail

Stuff the tail. Join the seam at the top as for the legs so it is straight; stitch it vertically to the back of the fox so it can swing from side to side.

This cheeky chap is crocheted in continuous rounds. His curly tail is shaped simply by increasing stitches on one side and decreasing on the other.

Monkey

monkey

DID YOU KNOW?
Groups of monkeys are
known as a "tribe," "troop,"
or "mission."

Information you'll need

Finished size

Approximately 16in (41cm) high

Materials

Adriafil Regina (or equivalent DK weight
yarn, CYCA 3), 100% merino wool
(137yds/125m per 50g ball)
2 x 50g balls in 016 Brown (A)
1 x 50g ball in 080 Mélange Light Beige (B)
C/2–D/3 (UK11:3mm) crochet hook
Darning needle
Toy stuffing
Embroidery needle
Stranded embroidery thread in black
Sewing needle
Black sewing thread
2 x black beads around ¼in (0.5cm)
in diameter

Gauge

24 sts and 28 rounds to 4in (10cm) over
single crochet using C/2–D/3 hook

Key

 Chain (ch)

• Slip stitch (sl st)

✛ Single crochet (sc)

✕✕ 2 sc in same st

✕✕ sc2tog

⊤ Half double (hdc)

⊤ Double crochet (dc)

V 2 dc in same st

Head

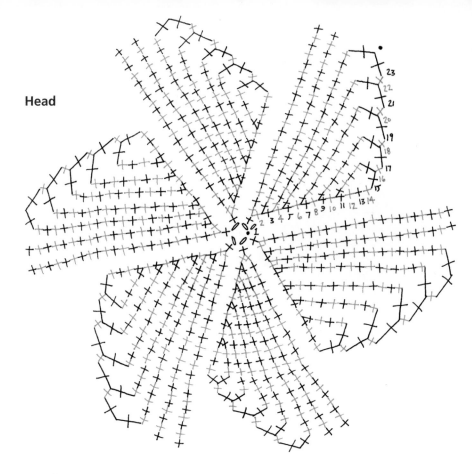

How to make Monkey

Monkey is of a similar style to Fox, with the body, bib, and legs made in the same way, so for charts see pages 52–59. Monkey is worked mainly in continuous rounds of single crochet, apart from the bib, which includes half double and double stitches. The pieces that form the face are crocheted separately and stitched on. The muzzle is stuffed to shape and the features are embroidered, with beads added for the eyes.

DID YOU KNOW?
Monkeys are most easily distinguished from apes by their tails—apes don't have any.

Head

Starting at the top of the head, with C/2–D/3 hook and A, make 4 ch and join with a sl st to the first ch to form a ring.
Round 1: 1 ch (does not count as a st), work 6 sc into ring (6 sts).
Round 2 (inc): (2 sc in next sc) 6 times (12 sts).
Round 3 (inc): (2 sc in next sc, 1 sc) 6 times (18 sts).
Round 4 (inc): (2 sc in next sc, 2 sc) 6 times (24 sts).
Round 5 (inc): (2 sc in next sc, 3 sc) 6 times (30 sts).
Round 6: Work 1 sc in each sc.
Round 7 (inc): (2 sc in next sc, 4 sc) 6 times (36 sts).
Round 8: Work 1 sc in each sc.
Round 9 (inc): (2 sc in next sc, 5 sc) 6 times (42 sts).

Round 10: Work 1 sc in each sc.
Round 11 (inc): (2 sc in next sc, 6 sc) 6 times (48 sts).
Rounds 12–14: Work 1 sc in each sc.
Round 15 (dec): (Sc2tog, 6 sc) 6 times (42 sts).
Round 16: Work 1 sc in each sc.
Round 17 (dec): (Sc2tog, 5 sc) 6 times (36 sts).
Round 18: Work 1 sc in each sc.
Round 19 (dec): (Sc2tog, 4 sc) 6 times (30 sts).
Round 20: Work 1 sc in each sc.
Round 21 (dec): (Sc2tog, 3 sc) 6 times (24 sts).
Round 22: Work 1 sc in each sc.
Round 23 (dec): (Sc2tog, 2 sc) 6 times (18 sts).
Sl st to the next st and fasten off, leaving a long length of yarn at the end.

Top of face

With C/2–D/3 hook and B, make 4 ch and join with a sl st to the first ch to form ring.

Round 1: 1 ch (does not count as a st), work 6 sc into ring (6 sts).

Round 2 (inc): (2 sc in next sc) 6 times (12 sts).

Round 3 (inc): (2 sc in next sc, 1 sc) 6 times (18 sts).

Round 4 (inc): (2 sc in next sc, 2 sc) 6 times (24 sts).

Round 5 (inc): (2 sc in next sc, 3 sc) 6 times (30 sts).

Round 6 (inc): (2 sc in next sc, 4 sc) 6 times (36 sts).

Round 7 (inc): (2 sc in next sc, 5 sc) 6 times (42 sts).

Round 8 (inc): Join A and work 1 sc in each sc.

Sl st to next st and fasten off, leaving a long length at the end.

Muzzle

With C/2–D/3 hook and B, make 4 ch and join with a sl st to the first ch to form a ring.

Round 1: 1 ch (does not count as a st), work 6 sc into ring (6 sts).

Round 2 (inc): (2 sc in next sc) 6 times (12 sts).

Round 3 (inc): (2 sc in next sc, 1 sc) 6 times (18 sts).

Round 4 (inc): (2 sc in next sc, 2 sc) 6 times (24 sts).

Round 5 (inc): (2 sc in next sc, 3 sc) 6 times (30 sts).

Round 6: Work 1 sc in each sc.

Round 7 (inc): (2 sc in next sc, 4 sc) 6 times (36 sts).

Rounds 8–9: Work 1 sc in each sc.
Sl st to next st and fasten off, leaving a long length at the end.

Body

With C/2–D/3 hook and A, make 4 ch and join with a sl st to the first ch to form a ring.

Round 1: 1 ch (does not count as a st), work 6 sc into ring (6 sts).

Round 2 (inc): (2 sc in next sc) 6 times (12 sts).

Round 3 (inc): (2 sc in next sc, 1 sc) 6 times (18 sts).

Round 4 (inc): (2 sc in next sc, 2 sc) 6 times (24 sts).

Round 5 (inc): (2 sc in next sc, 3 sc) 6 times (30 sts).

Round 6 (inc): (2 sc in next sc, 4 sc) 6 times (36 sts).

Round 7 (inc): (2 sc in next sc, 5 sc) 6 times (42 sts).

Rounds 8–10: Work 1 sc in each sc.

Round 11 (dec): (Sc2tog, 5 sc) 6 times (36 sts).

Rounds 12–14: Work 1 sc in each sc.

Round 15 (dec): (Sc2tog, 4 sc) 6 times (30 sts).

Rounds 16–20: Work 1 sc in each sc.

Round 21 (dec): (Sc2tog, 3 sc) 6 times (24 sts).

Rounds 22–26: Work 1 sc in each sc.

Round 27 (dec): (Sc2tog, 2 sc) 6 times (18 sts).

Rounds 28–32: Work 1 sc in each sc.
Sl st to next st and fasten off, leaving a long length of yarn.

Note: Monkey's body is the same as Fox's; for chart see page 55.

Top of face

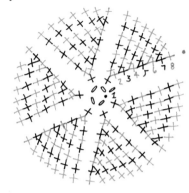

Muzzle

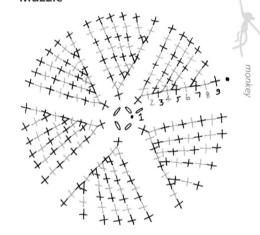

monkey

63

Bib

With C/2–D/3 hook and B, make 19 ch.
Round 1: 1 sc into second ch from hook, 1 sc in next 16 ch, 3 sc in end ch, 1 sc in reverse side of each ch to end (37 sts).
Round 2 (inc): 2 ch, 1 sc in next 8 sc, 1 hdc in next 4 sc, 1 dc in next 4 sc, (2 dc in same st) 5 times, 1 dc in next 4 sc, 1 hdc in next 4 sc, 1 sc in next 8 sc (42 sts and one 2 ch sp).
Round 3 (inc): Work 3 sc in the 2 ch sp, 1 sc in each of next 8 sc, 1 sc in each of next 4 hdc, 1 sc in each of next 4 dc, 2 sc in each of next 10 dc, 1 sc in each of next 4 dc, 1 sc in each of next 4 hdc, 1 sc in next 8 sc (55 sts).
Sl st to next st and fasten off, leaving a long length of yarn. **Note:** Monkey's bib is the same as Fox's; for chart see page 56.

Inner ears (make 2)

With C/2–D/3 hook and B, make 4 ch and join with a sl st to the first ch to form ring.
Row 1: 1 ch (does not count as a st), work 6 sc into ring (6 sts).
Row 2 (inc): (2 sc in next sc) 6 times (12 sts).
Row 3 (inc): (2 sc in next sc, 1 sc) 6 times (18 sts).
Row 4 (inc): (2 sc in next sc, 2 sc) 6 times (24 sts). Sl st to next st and fasten off.

Outer ears (make 2)

With C/2–D/3 hook and A, make 4 ch and join with a sl st to the first ch to form a ring. Work rounds 1–4 as for the inner ears. Do not fasten off at the end.

Join ear pieces

Place the ear pieces together with the inner piece facing you. Using C/2–D/3 hook and yarn A, join the inner and outer ear pieces by working 1 sc in each of the next 24 sc of both pieces at the same time, inserting hook under both loops of each stitch. Sl st to next st and fasten off, leaving a long length. Weave in short ends.

Arms (make 2)

With C/2–D/3 hook and B, make 4 ch and join with a sl st to form a ring.
Round 1: 1 ch (does not count as a st), work 6 sc into ring (6 sts).
Round 2 (inc): (2 sc in next sc) 6 times (12 sts).
Rounds 3–7: Work 1 sc in each sc. Join and continue in A.
Next: Work 1 sc in each sc until arm measures 7in (18cm).
Sl st to next st and fasten off.

Legs (make 2)

With C/2–D/3 hook and B, make 4 ch and join with a sl st to form a ring.
Work rounds 1–7 as for the arms.
Join and continue in A.
Next: Work 1 sc in each sc until leg measures 8⅝in (22cm).
Sl st to next st and fasten off.
Note: Monkey's arms and legs are the same as Fox's legs; for chart see page 57.

Tail

With C/2–D/3 hook and A, make 4 ch and join with a sl st to form a ring.
Round 1: 1 ch (does not count as a st), work 6 sc into ring (6 sts).
Round 2 (inc): (2 sc in next sc) 6 times (12 sts)
Rounds 3–4: Work 1 sc in each sc.
Shape tail
Round 5: Sc2tog, 1 sc in next 3 sc, (2 sc in next sc) twice, 1 sc in next 3 sc, sc2tog. This will put a curl in the tail. Repeat round 5 until the tail measures around 8in (20cm).
Sl st to next st and fasten off, leaving a long length of yarn.

Ears

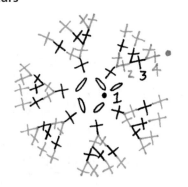

Join ear pieces

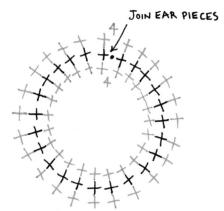

Tail

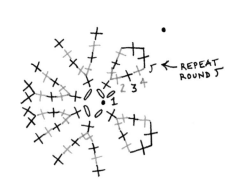

Finishing

Head

Using a blunt-ended darning needle, weave the yarn through the last round of stitches of the head, then stuff firmly before drawing up the yarn to close the opening and stitch together to secure.

Face

Sew the circular-shaped top of the face using the long length of A, positioning it above the center, toward the top of the head. Use the long length of yarn left after fastening off the muzzle to stitch it over the top of the face and toward the bottom of the head. It might help to pin it in position first. Leave a small opening and push some stuffing through to shape the muzzle before stitching it down. Embroider the eyelashes in straight stitch with three strands of black embroidery thread, then sew the beads on for the eyes. Alternatively, work a French knot for each eye. Embroider the nostrils in satin stitch, using three strands of embroidery thread and working just two or three stitches for each one.

Ears

With the long length of yarn left, sew the ears in place on each side of the head, stitching well in front and behind the ear to keep them firmly in place.

Body

Stuff the body firmly. Use a darning needle to weave the length of yarn left at the end through the last round of stitches, draw up to gather and work a few stitches over each other to fasten off.

Bib

Use the length of yarn left at the end of the bib to sew it to the front of the body with the narrow end at the neck. Stitch the head to the body, sewing all around the neck to join securely and prevent it from flopping about.

Arms/Legs

Stuff the arms and legs. Stitch the top end of each limb by squeezing it together and sewing the stitches from each side to form a straight seam. Sew the seam at the top of the arms in place along the neckline and stitch the legs to the lower end of the body.

Tail

Stuff the tail, keeping the curly shape. Join the seam at the top as for the arms and legs so it is straight, then stitch it vertically to the back of the monkey so it can swing from side to side.

monkey

The pattern on the snake's body is produced by working into consecutive rows, but it can be crocheted in stripes for a more simple design. This snake is so long, it would make a great draft stopper!

Snake

GULP!
Snakes have flexible jaws, which allow them to swallow prey bigger than their heads. This makes being a snake dentist a hazardous job.

Information you'll need

Finished size
Approximately 1¾yds (1.6m) head to tail

Materials
King Cole Merino Blend DK (or equivalent DK weight yarn, CYCA 3), 100% wool (123yds/112m per 50g ball)
2 x 50g balls in 925 Beige (A)
1 x 50g balls in 796 Beech (B)
1 x 50g balls in 023 Chocolate (C)
Scraps of DK yarn in pink and deep red
B/1–C/2 (UK12:2.5mm) and C/2–D/3 (UK11:3mm) crochet hooks
Darning needle
Toy stuffing
Sewing needle
Black sewing thread
2 x black beads around ¼in (0.5cm) in diameter

Gauge
22 sts and 24 rounds to 4in (10cm) over single crochet using C/2–D/3 hook

Key

∂ Chain (ch)

• Slip stitch (sl st)

+ Single crochet (sc)

⟩⟨ 2 sc in same st

⟩⟨ sc2tog

⟩⟨ 3sc in next st

Jaw
Rows 1–9
Mouth
Work rows 1–6 only

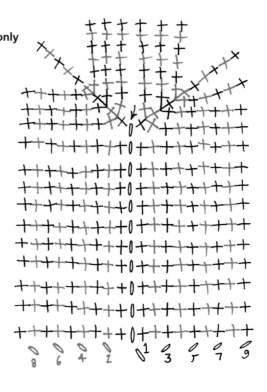

How to make Snake

The jaw and mouth are crocheted in pieces and joined to form the finished head. The body starts at the tail; this is increased gradually, working in continuous rounds of single crochet with the pattern forming the snakeskin. The body is stuffed as the work grows in length. The neck is shaped by decreasing stitches and the head is sewn on to the open end. The tongue is made in rows of single crochet and slip stitch and sewn into the mouth. Beads for eyes finish the features.

Head

Jaw

With C/2–D/3 hook and A, make 12 ch.
Row 1: 1 sc into second ch from hook, 1 sc into the next 9 ch, 2 sc into end ch, 1 sc into each of the reverse side of the next 10 ch, turn (22 sts).
Row 2 (inc) (RS): 1 ch (does not count as a st), 10 sc, (3 sc into next sc) twice, 10 sc, turn (26 sts).
Row 3 (inc): 1 ch (does not count as a st), 11 sc, 3 sc into next sc, 2 sc, 3 sc into next sc, 11 sc, turn (30 sts).

Row 4 (inc): 1 ch (does not count as a st), 12 sc, 3 sc into next sc, 4 sc, 3 sc into next sc, 12 sc, turn (34 sts).
Rows 5–9: 1 ch (does not count as a st), work 1 sc in each sc, turn.
Fasten off.
Make one more piece to match the first.

Back of head

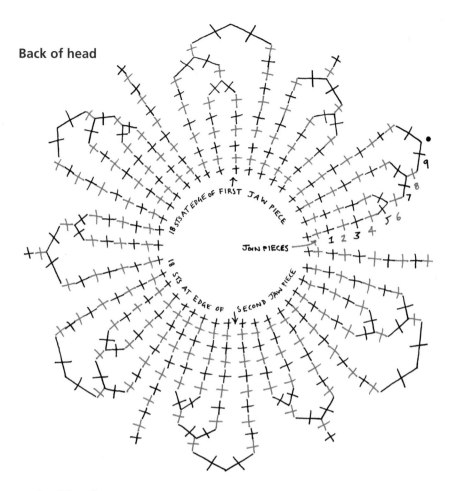

18 STS AT EDGE OF FIRST JAW PIECE

JOIN PIECES

18 STS AT EDGE OF SECOND JAW PIECE

1 2 3 4 5 6 7 8 9

Attach mouth

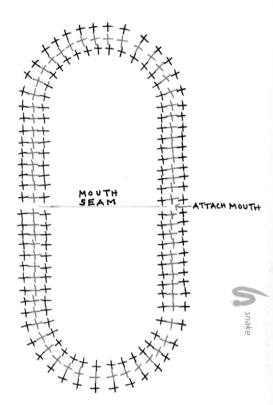

MOUTH SEAM

ATTACH MOUTH

snake

Back of head

With right side facing, C/2–D/3 hook and A, work 18 sc evenly across the straight edge of the first jaw piece and continue across the second jaw piece to join (36 sts). The following is worked in rounds:
Round 1 (inc): 1 sc into the first sc to join the other ends of each jaw piece, 1 sc into each of the next 35 sc.
Rounds 2–4: Work 1 sc in each sc.
Shape back of head
Round 5 (dec): (Sc2tog, 2 sc) 9 times (27 sts).
Round 6: Work 1 sc in each sc.
Round 7 (dec): (Sc2tog, 1 sc) 9 times (18 sts).

Round 8: Work 1 sc in each sc.
Round 9 (dec): (Sc2tog, 1 sc) 6 times (12 sts).
Sl st to the next st and fasten off, leaving a long length of yarn at the end.

Mouth

With C/2–D/3 hook and DK yarn in pink, make two pieces as for the jaw, working rows 1–6 only.
Next: With right sides together, stitch along the straight edges to join.

Attach mouth

With C/2–D/3 hook and A, join the yarn to the pink mouth at the edge of the seam just stitched. With wrong sides together, match the stitches of both the mouth and jaw pieces. Insert the hook under both loops of the first sc of the mouth first, then under both loops of the first sc of the jaw and work 1 sc to join the two stitches. Continue in this way, working together each of the 68 sc from both pieces at the same time, being sure to insert the hook into a single crochet of the mouth first and then the jaw. Fasten off.

Body

Starting at the tail end, with C/2–D/3 hook and A, wind yarn around a finger a few times to form a ring, insert the hook, catch the yarn and draw back through the ring.

Round 1: 1 ch (does not count as a st), work 6 sc into ring (6 sts).

Round 2: Work 1 sc in each sc.

Round 3 (inc): (2 sc in next sc, 1 sc) 3 times. Pull on short end to close the ring (9 sts).

Rounds 4–6: Work 1 sc in each sc.

Round 7 (inc): (2 sc in next sc, 2 sc) 3 times (12 sts).

Rounds 8–10: Work 1 sc in each sc.

Round 11 (inc): (2 sc in next sc, 3 sc) 3 times (15 sts).

Rounds 12–15: Work 1 sc in each sc.

Round 16 (inc): (2 sc in next sc, 4 sc) 3 times (18 sts).

Rounds 17–20: Work 1 sc in each sc.

Round 21 (inc): (2 sc in next sc, 5 sc) 3 times (21 sts).

Rounds 22–25: Work 1 sc in each sc.

Round 26 (inc): (2 sc in next sc, 6 sc) 3 times (24 sts).

Rounds 27–30: Work 1 sc in each sc.

Round 31 (inc): (2 sc in next sc, 7 sc) 3 times (27 sts).

Rounds 32–35: Work 1 sc in each sc.

Round 36 (inc): (2 sc in next sc, 8 sc) 3 times (30 sts).

Rounds 37–40: Work 1 sc in each sc.

Tail
Rounds 1–20

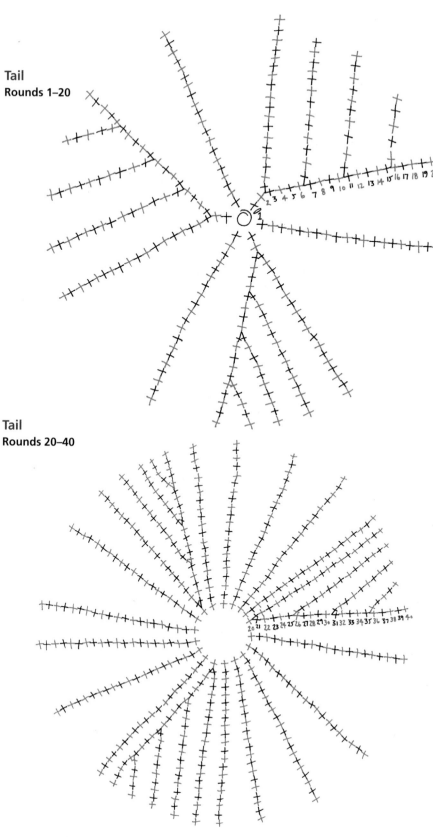

Tail
Rounds 20–40

Crocheted Wild Animals

Pattern

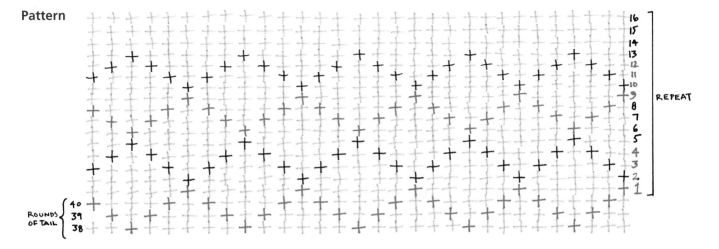

ROUNDS OF TAIL { 40 39 38

16 15 14 13 12 11 10 9 8 7 6 5 4 3 2 1 } REPEAT

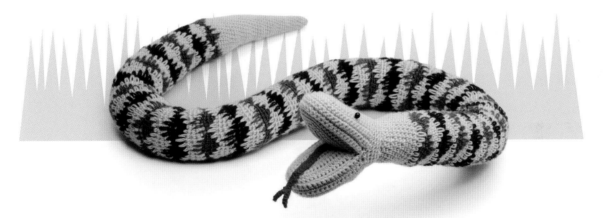

Pattern

Note: As the stitches are made by missing rows, the loop on the hook should be extended up to the level of the row being worked. Join the next color by inserting the hook into the next sc, then catch A and draw back through the stitch (2 loops on hook), catch B and draw through both loops on the hook.

Round 1: With B, (1 sc into the next sc, 1 sc into the next sc 1 row down, 1 sc into the next sc 2 rows down, 1 sc into the next sc 3 rows down, 1 sc into the next sc 2 rows down, 1 sc into the next sc 1 row down) 5 times.

Rounds 2–4: Work 1 sc into each sc. Finish the last round 1 st before the first sc on round 1 of the pattern.

Join the next color by inserting the hook into the next sc, then catch yarn B and draw back through the stitch (2 loops on hook), catch yarn A and draw through both loops on the hook.

Round 5: With A, (1 sc into the next sc 3 rows down, 1 sc into the next sc 2 rows down, 1 sc into the next sc 1 row down, 1 sc into the next sc, 1 sc into the next sc 1 row down, 1 sc into the next sc 2 rows down) 5 times.

Rounds 6–8: Work 1 sc into each sc. Finish the last round 1 st before the first sc on round 5 of the pattern.

Join C in the same way as before.

Rounds 9–12: As rounds 1–4 in C.

Rounds 13–16: As rounds 5–8 in A. These 16 rounds form the pattern of the snake's body. Repeat these rounds 15 more times, then rounds 1–8 once more, finishing with yarn A.

Stuff the body as you work every 8–12in (20–30cm), but not too firmly.

Tongue

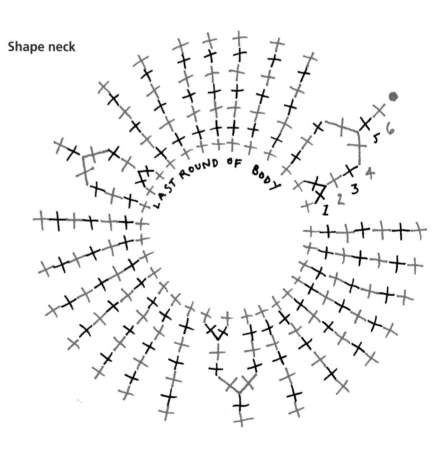

Shape neck

Round 1 (dec): (Sc2tog, 8 sc) 3 times
(27 sts).
Rounds 2–3: Work 1 sc in each sc.
Round 4 (dec): (Sc2tog, 7 sc) 3 times
(24 sts).
Rounds 5–6: Work 1 sc in each sc.
Sl st to next st, leaving a long length of
yarn at the end.

Tongue

With B/1–C/2 hook and DK yarn in red,
make 30 ch, leaving a long length of yarn
at the beginning.
Row 1: Sl st into second ch from hook, sl
st into next 4 ch, 1 sc into each of the next
24 ch, turn (24 sts).
Row 2 (RS): Sl st into each of the next
24 sc, turn.
Row 3: Make 6 ch, sl st into second ch
from hook, sl st into next 4 ch, sl st into
next st and fasten off.

Shape neck

LAST ROUND OF BODY

DID YOU KNOW?
There is nothing inside the rattlesnake's rattle; the noise comes from the tail segments knocking together.

snake

Finishing

Head

Stuff the head, filling the upper and lower jaw, but keeping the pink inside of the mouth flat. Thread the yarn length left after shaping the back of the head through the last round of stitches, gather up the opening and stitch to secure.

Body

Stuff the rest of the body, filling it right up to the edge of the neck. With the length of yarn left after fastening off, sew the body to the head, stitching all around the neck edge and adding a little extra stuffing if necessary before closing.

Tongue

Weave in the ends of the tongue. Using the length of yarn left at the beginning, stitch to the inside of the mouth to the center of the seam joining the two mouth pieces. Sew the beads in place for the eyes. Alternatively, embroider French knots using DK yarn in black for the eyes.

The yarn used for this lop-eared rabbit has a lovely natural look and texture.
If you are making the project for a baby, choose a softer, less fibrous yarn,
such as Debbie Bliss Baby Cashmerino.

Rabbit

Information you'll need

Finished size
Approximately 11¼in (28.5cm) high (not including the ears)

Materials
Bergère de France Lima (or equivalent Sport weight yarn, CYCA 2), 80% wool, 20% alpaca (120yds/110m per 50g ball)
2 x 50g balls in 22507 Steppe (A)
1 x 50g ball in 22890 Aurore (B)
1 x 50g ball in 20441 Polaire (C)
B/1–C/2 (UK12:2.5mm) and C/2–D/3 (UK11:3mm) crochet hooks
Darning needle
Toy stuffing
Knitting needle or pencil to aid in stuffing rabbit
Embroidery needle
Stranded embroidery thread in black
Air-erasable fabric marker or tailor's chalk pencil

Gauge
26 sts and 28 rounds to 4in (10cm) over single crochet using C/2–D/3 hook

rabbit

Key

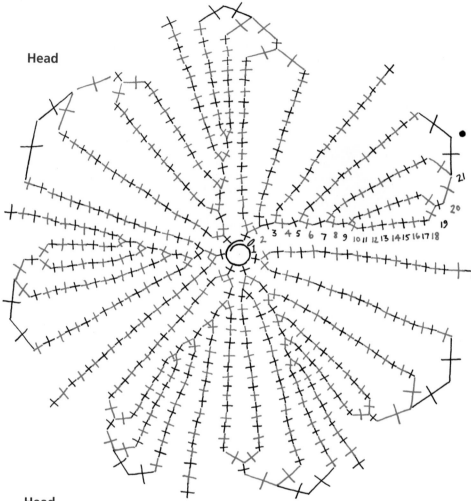

🜉 Wind yarn around finger to form ring

⊖ Chain (ch)

• Slip stitch (sl st)

+ Single crochet (sc)

XX 2 sc in same st

XX sc2tog

XↃ 3 sc in same st

⊤ sc into back loop

⊥ sc into front loop

XↃ 2 sc in same st into front loop

↶XↃ sc2tog into front loops

↗ Start

Head

How to make Rabbit

The head, body, arms, and legs are worked in continuous rounds of single crochet. The ears are made in two pieces, both worked in rows of single crochet, but using a smaller hook for the inner ears. The fluffy tail is worked in a chain loop stitch. A pompom can be attached as an alternative to the crocheted tail. The features are embroidered in chain stitch, straight stitch, and cross stitch.

Head

Starting at the nose, with C/2–D/3 hook and A, wind yarn around a finger a few times to form a ring, insert the hook, catch the yarn and draw back through the ring.
Round 1: Make 1 ch (does not count as a st), work 6 sc into ring (6 sts).
Round 2 (inc): (2 sc in next sc) 6 times, pull on short end to close ring (12 sts).
Round 3 (inc): (2 sc in next sc, 3 sc) 3 times (15 sts).
Round 4 (inc): (2 sc in next sc, 2 sc) 5 times (20 sts).
Round 5: Work 1 sc in each sc.
Round 6 (inc): (2 sc in next sc, 3 sc) 5 times (25 sts).

Round 7: Work 1 sc in each sc.
Round 8 (inc): (2 sc in next sc, 4 sc) 5 times (30 sts).
Round 9: Work 1 sc in each sc.
Round 10 (inc): (2 sc in next sc, 5 sc) 5 times (35 sts).
Rounds 11–17: Work 1 sc in each sc.
Round 18 (dec): (Sc2tog, 3 sc) 7 times (28 sts).
Round 19: Work 1 sc in each sc.
Round 20 (dec): (Sc2tog, 2 sc) 7 times (21 sts).
Round 21 (dec): (Sc2tog, 1 sc) 7 times (14 sts). Sl st to next sc and fasten off, leaving a long length of yarn.

Body

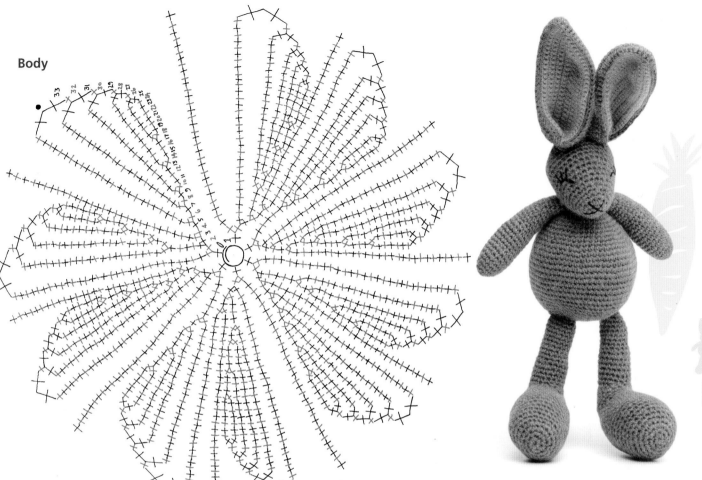

rabbit

Body

Starting at the top of the body, with C/2–D/3 hook and A, wind yarn around a finger a couple of times to form a ring, insert the hook, catch the yarn and draw back through the ring.

Round 1: Make 1 ch (does not count as a st), work 6 sc into ring (6 sts).

Round 2 (inc): (2 sc in next sc) 6 times, pull on short end to close ring (12 sts).

Round 3 (inc): (2 sc in next sc, 1 sc) 6 times (18 sts).

Round 4 (inc): (2 sc in next sc, 2 sc) 6 times (24 sts).

Round 5: Work 1 sc in each sc.

Round 6 (inc): (2 sc in next sc, 3 sc) 6 times (30 sts).

Round 7: Work 1 sc in each sc.

Round 8 (inc): (2 sc in next sc, 2 sc) 10 times (40 sts).

Round 9: Work 1 sc in each sc.

Round 10 (inc): (2 sc in next sc, 3 sc) 10 times (50 sts).

Rounds 11–13: Work 1 sc in each sc.

Round 14 (inc): (2 sc in next sc, 4 sc) 10 times (60 sts).

Rounds 15–17: Work 1 sc in each sc.

Round 18 (inc): (2 sc in next sc, 5 sc) 10 times (70 sts).

Rounds 19–24: Work 1 sc in each sc.

Round 25 (dec): (Sc2tog, 5 sc) 10 times (60 sts).

Round 26: Work 1 sc in each sc.

Round 27 (dec): (Sc2tog, 4 sc) 10 times (50 sts).

Round 28: Work 1 sc in each sc.

Round 29 (dec): (Sc2tog, 3 sc) 10 times (40 sts).

Round 30: Work 1 sc in each sc.

Round 31 (dec): (Sc2tog, 2 sc) 10 times (30 sts).

Round 32: Work 1 sc in each sc.

Round 33 (dec): (Sc2tog, 1 sc) 10 times (20 sts).

Sl st to next sc and fasten off, leaving a long length of yarn.

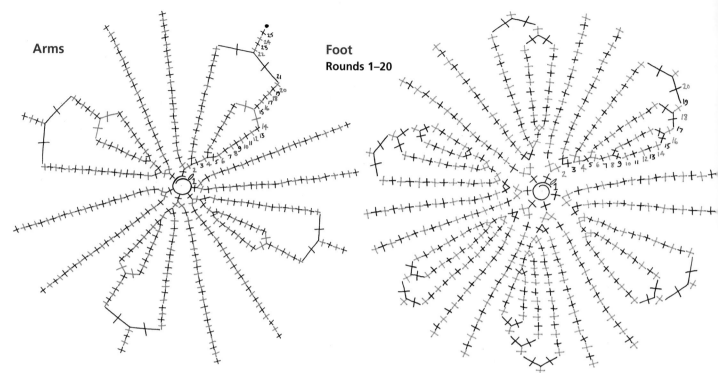

Arms

Foot
Rounds 1–20

Arms (make 2)

Starting at the paw, with C/2–D/3 hook and A, wind yarn around a finger a couple of times to form a ring, insert the hook, catch the yarn and draw back through the ring.

Round 1: Make 1 ch (does not count as a st), work 6 sc into ring (6 sts).

Round 2 (inc): (2 sc in next sc) 6 times, pull on short end to close ring (12 sts).

Round 3 (inc): (2 sc in next sc, 2 sc) 4 times (16 sts).

Round 4: Work 1 sc in each sc.

Round 5 (inc): (2 sc in next sc, 3 sc) 4 times (20 sts).

Rounds 6–13: Work 1 sc in each sc.

Round 14 (dec): (Sc2tog, 3 sc) 4 times (16 sts).

Rounds 15–20: Work 1 sc in each sc.

Round 21 (dec): (Sc2tog, 2 sc) 4 times (12 sts).

Rounds 22–25: Work 1 sc in each sc. Sl st to next sc and fasten off, leaving a long length of yarn.

Legs (make 2)
Foot

Starting at the toe, with C/2–D/3 hook and A, wind yarn around a finger a couple of times to form a ring, insert the hook, catch the yarn and draw back through the ring.

Round 1: Make 1 ch (does not count as a st), work 6 sc into ring (6 sts).

Round 2 (inc): (2 sc in next sc) 6 times, pull on short end to close ring (12 sts)

Round 3 (inc): (2 sc in next sc, 1 sc) 6 times (18 sts).

Round 4 (inc): (2 sc in next sc, 2 sc) 6 times (24 sts).

Round 5: Work 1 sc in each sc.

Round 6 (inc): (2 sc in next sc, 3 sc) 6 times (30 sts).

Rounds 7–8: Work 1 sc in each sc.

Round 9 (inc): (2 sc in next sc, 9 sc) 3 times (33 sts).

Rounds 10–14: Work 1 sc in each sc.

Round 15 (dec): (Sc2tog, 9 sc) 3 times (30 sts).

Round 16: Work 1 sc in each sc.

Round 17 (dec): (Sc2tog, 3 sc) 6 times (24 sts).

Round 18: Work 1 sc in each sc.

Round 19 (dec): (Sc2tog, 2 sc) 6 times (18 sts).

Round 20: Work 1 sc in each sc.

DID YOU KNOW?
Rabbits enjoy a supermodel diet of fruit and vegetables.

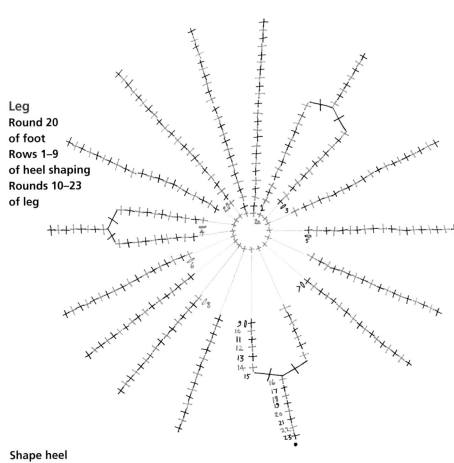

Leg
Round 20
of foot
Rows 1–9
of heel shaping
Rounds 10–23
of leg

HE'S BEHIND YOU!
Rabbits have a 360° field of vision, so can see things behind them without turning around. Makes creeping up on them no fun.

rabbit

Shape heel
The following is worked in rows:
Row 1: 1 sc in next 2 sc, turn (2 sts).
Row 2: 1 ch (does not count as a stitch), work 1 sc into the sc in front of the first sc, 1 sc in next 3 sc, turn (4 sts).
Row 3: 1 ch (does not count as a stitch), work 1 sc into the sc in front of the first sc, 1 sc in next 5 sc, turn (6 sts).
Row 4: 1 ch (does not count as a stitch), work 1 sc into the sc in front of the first sc, 1 sc in next 7 sc, turn (8 sts).
Row 5: 1 ch (does not count as a stitch), work 1 sc into the sc in front of the first sc, 1 sc in next 9 sc, turn (10 sts).
Row 6: 1 ch (does not count as a stitch), work 1 sc into the sc in front of the first sc, 1 sc in next 11 sc, turn (12 sts).
Row 7: 1 ch (does not count as a stitch), work 1 sc into the sc in front of the first sc, 1 sc in next 13 sc, turn (14 sts).

Row 8: 1 ch (does not count as a stitch), work 1 sc into the sc in front of the first sc, 1 sc in next 15 sc, turn (16 sts).
Row 9: 1 ch (does not count as a stitch), work 1 sc into the sc in front of the first sc, 1 sc in next 17 sc, do not turn at end (18 sts).
The following is worked in rounds:
Work 5 continuous rounds of 1 sc in each sc.
Round 15 (dec): (Sc2tog, 4 sc) 3 times (15 sts).
Rounds 16–23: Work 1 sc in each sc. Sl st in next st and fasten off, leaving a length of yarn.

Outer ear and inner ear

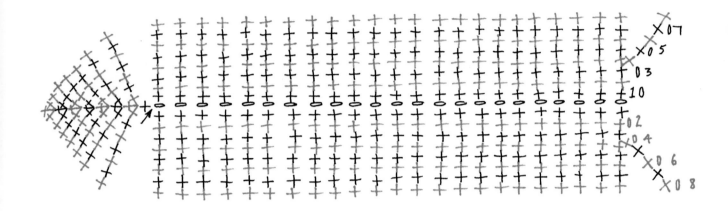

Outer ears (make 2)

With C/2–D/3 hook and A, make 24 ch.

Row 1 (WS): 1 sc into second ch from hook, 1 sc into next 21 ch, 3 sc into next ch, 1 sc down reverse side of ch to end, turn (47 sts).

Row 2 (inc) (RS): 1 ch (does not count as a st), 23 sc, 3 sc in next sc, 23 sc, turn (49 sts).

Row 3 (inc): 1 ch (does not count as a st), 24 sc, 3 sc in next sc, 24 sc, turn (51 sts).

Row 4 (inc): 1 ch (does not count as a st), 2 sc in next sc, 24 sc, 3 sc in next sc, 24 sc, 2 sc in next sc, turn (55 sts).

Row 5 (inc): 1 ch (does not count as a st), 27 sc, 3 sc in next sc, 27 sc, turn (57 sts).

Row 6 (inc): 1 ch (does not count as a st), 28 sc, 3 sc in next sc, 28 sc, turn (59 sts).

Row 7 (inc): 1 ch (does not count as a st), 29 sc, 3 sc in next sc, 29 sc, turn (61 sts).

Row 8 (inc): 1 ch (does not count as a st), 30 sc, 3 sc in next sc, 30 sc (63 sts). Fasten off.

Inner ears (make 2)

With B/1–C/2 hook and B, make 24 ch. Work rows 1–8 of outer ear. Fasten off.

Join ear pieces

Place the wrong sides of the ear pieces together with the inner piece facing you. Using C/2–D/3 hook and yarn A, join the inner and outer ear pieces by working 1 sc in each sc of both ear pieces at the same time, inserting the hook under both loops of each stitch. You will find the stitches of the inner ear a little tight as they were made using the smaller hook. Fasten off, leaving a long length. Weave in the short ends.

Tail

The loops will appear at the back of the fabric as you work. With C/2–D/3 hook and C, wind yarn around a finger a few times to form a ring, insert the hook, catch the yarn and draw back through the ring.

Round 1: Make 1 ch (does not count as a st), work 6 sc into ring (6 sts).

Round 2: (6 ch, 1 sc into back loop only) 6 times (6 loops).

Round 3 (inc): (2 sc in next sc into front loop only of the stitches in round 1) 6 times, sl st to next st, pull on short end of yarn to close ring (12 sts).

Round 4: (6 ch, 1 sc) into back loop only of each sc of previous round (12 loops).

Round 5: Work 1 sc into front loop only of each sc of round 3, sl st to next st.

Round 6: (6 ch, 1 sc) into back loop only of each sc of previous round (12 loops).

Round 7 (inc): (2 sc in next sc into front loop only of the stitches in round 5) 12 times, sl st to next st (24 sts).

Round 8: (6 ch, 1 sc) into back loop only of each sc of previous round (24 loops).

Round 9: Work 1 sc into front loop only of each sc of round 7, sl st to next st.

Round 10: (6 ch, 1 sc) into back loop only of each sc of previous round (24 loops).

Round 11 (dec): (Sc2tog into front loop only of the stitches in round 9) 12 times, sl st to next st (12 sts).

Round 12: (6 ch, 1 sc) into back loop only of each sc of previous round (12 loops).

Round 13: Work 1 sc into front loop only of each sc of round 11 (12 sts).

Round 14: Work 1 sc into both loops of each sc, sl st to next st and fasten off, leaving a long length of yarn.

Tail

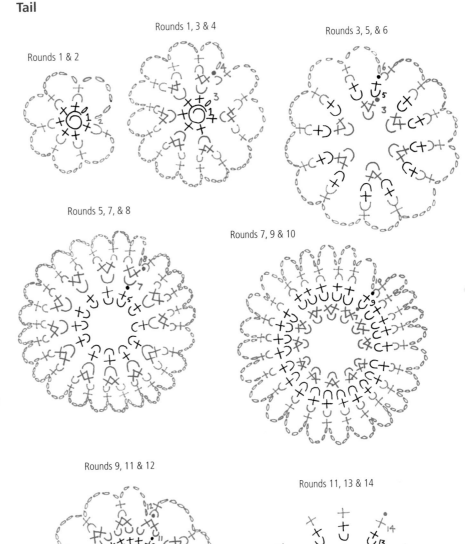

Rounds 1 & 2

Rounds 1, 3 & 4

Rounds 3, 5, & 6

Rounds 5, 7, & 8

Rounds 7, 9 & 10

Rounds 9, 11 & 12

Rounds 11, 13 & 14

rabbit

81

Finishing

Head

Stuff the head firmly with toy stuffing. Thread the yarn onto a needle and run a gathering stitch around the last round of stitches, draw up to close and fasten off.

Ears

Sew the lower edges of the inner and outer ear pieces together to join. Bring the two corners at each side of the lower edge of the ear to the middle and stitch together to shape, with the pink inner piece on the inside. Run a gathering stitch around the lower edge of the ear, draw up and secure with a few stitches before sewing in place on the head.

Body

Stuff the body firmly and run a gathering stitch around the last round of stitches. Draw up to close and fasten off. Sew the head in place on top of the body.

Arms

Stuff the arms, just enough to fill them but still keeping them soft. Thread the fastened-off length of yarn onto a needle, gather the opening and draw up to close. Attach an arm to each side of the rabbit, stitching it securely between the head and body.

Feet

Stuff the feet firmly, using a knitting needle or the end of a pencil to push the stuffing right into the end of the foot and the heel. Stuff the leg, a little less firmly, filling it to the top. Thread the fastened-off length of yarn onto a needle and run a gathering stitch around the last round of stitches, then draw up to close. Sew the legs to the base of the body, slightly off-center toward the front, working the stitches securely all around the top of the leg and into the body.

Tail

Stuff the tail, thread the fastened-off length of yarn onto a needle and run a line of stitches through the last round of single crochet. Draw up the stitches to close the open end. Sew the gathered end of the tail in position on the body.

Eyes

Mark the position of the eyes with an air-erasable fabric marker or tailor's chalk pencil. With four strands of black embroidery thread, embroider the curved eye line in chain stitch and three eyelashes in straight stitch. Embroider the nose in a large cross stitch.

RUN TO THE BEAT

Rabbits thump their back legs to warn other rabbits in the area of danger. This is why rabbits never throw bongo-playing parties.

This pattern can be adapted to make a lioness simply by leaving out the mane.
She would make a lovely companion for this friendly lion.

Lion

lion

DID YOU KNOW?
Lions can reach speeds of up to 50mph (81km/h) but only in short bursts. They don't have the stamina to run marathons and can't find running shoes to fit them anyway.

Information you'll need

Finished size
Approximately 11½in (29cm) from nose to tail

Materials
King Cole Merino Blend DK (or equivalent DK weight yarn, CYCA 3), 100% wool (123yds/112m per 50g ball)
3 x 50g balls in 855 Mustard (A)
Scraps of DK yarn in cream or white (B) and black (C)
B/1–C/2 (UK12:2.5mm) and C/2–D/3 (UK11:3mm) crochet hooks
Darning needle
Toy stuffing
Embroidery needle

Gauge
22 sts and 24 rounds to 4in (10cm) over single crochet using C/2–D/3 hook

Key

⊙ Wind yarn around finger to form a ring

⟋ Chain (ch)

• Slip stitch (sl st)

+ Single crochet (sc)

⤬⤬ 2 sc in same st

⤬⤬ sc2tog

⟓ Single crochet into back loop only

⟓ Slip stitch into back loop of single crochet and the chain at the same time to join

Head

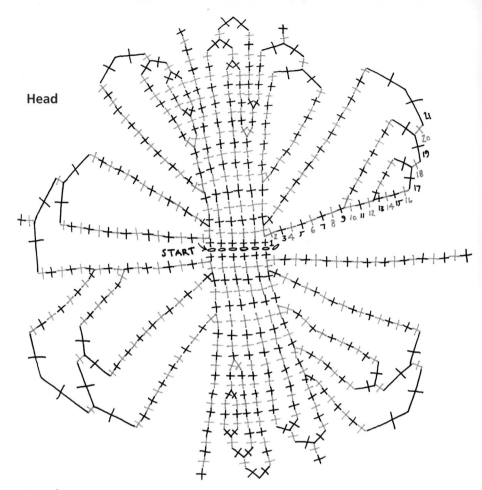

How to make Lion

Each piece is worked in rounds of single crochet and stitched together to form the lion. The shaping is done by increasing and decreasing stitches. The mane and the tassel at the end of the tail are made of loops of chain stitches joined back into the work with a single crochet or slip stitch. The eyes are embroidered in French knots, but can be replaced with buttons or beads for an alternative finish.

Head

With C/2–D/3 hook and B, make 7 ch.
Round 1: Starting under the chin, work 1 sc into second ch from hook, 1 sc into the next 4 ch, 2 sc into end ch, 1 sc into each of the reverse side of the next 5 ch (12 sts).
Round 2 (inc): 2 sc in next sc, 1 sc into next 4 sc, (2 sc in next sc) twice, 1 sc into next 4 sc, 2 sc in next sc (16 sts).
Round 3 (inc): 1 sc into next sc, 2 sc in next sc, 1 sc into next 4 sc, 2 sc in next sc, 1 sc into next 2 sc, 2 sc in next sc, 1 sc into next 4 sc, 2 sc in next sc,1 sc in next sc (20 sts).
Rounds 4–5: Work 1 sc in each sc. Join and continue in A.
Round 6 (inc): 1 sc into next 2 sc, (2 sc in next sc, 4 sc) 3 times, 2 sc in next sc, 1 sc into next 2 sc (24 sts).

Rounds 7–9: Work 1 sc in each sc.
Round 10 (inc): (2 sc in next sc, 3 sc) 6 times (30 sts).
Rounds 11–12: Work 1 sc in each sc.
Round 13 (inc): (2 sc in next sc, 4 sc) 6 times (36 sts).
Rounds 14–16: Work 1 sc in each sc.
Shape back of head
Round 17 (dec): (Sc2tog, 2 sc) 9 times (27 sts).
Round 18: Work 1 sc in each sc.
Round 19 (dec): (Sc2tog, 1 sc) 9 times (18 sts).
Round 20: Work 1 sc in each sc.
Round 21 (dec): (Sc2tog, 1 sc) 6 times (12 sts). Break yarn and thread through the last round of stitches, stuff the head firmly, gather up the opening and stitch to secure.

Body
Rounds 1–42

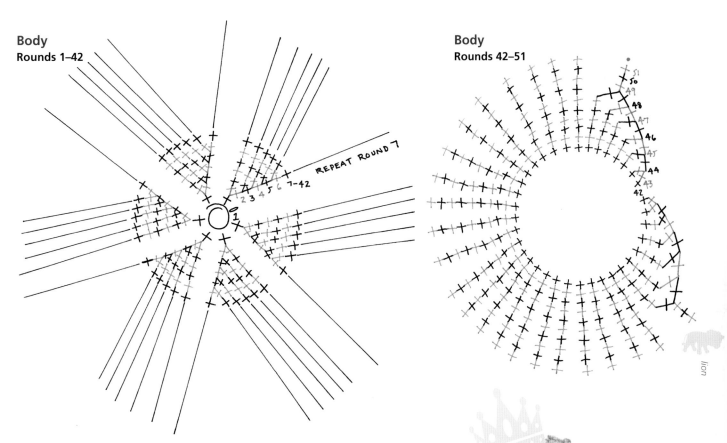

Body
Rounds 42–51

REPEAT ROUND 7

1 2 3 4 5 6 7-42

42 43 44 45 46 47 48 49 50 51

lion

Body

Starting at the tail end of the lion, with C/2–D/3 hook and A, wind yarn around a finger a couple of times to form a ring, insert the hook, catch the yarn and draw back through the ring.

Round 1: 1 ch (does not count as a st), work 6 sc into ring (6 sts).

Round 2 (inc): (2 sc in next sc) 6 times. Pull on short end to close ring (12 sts).

Round 3 (inc): (2 sc in next sc, 1 sc) 6 times (18 sts).

Round 4 (inc): (2 sc in next sc, 2 sc) 6 times (24 sts).

Round 5 (inc): (2 sc in next sc, 3 sc) 6 times (30 sts).

Round 6 (inc): (2 sc in next sc, 4 sc) 6 times (36 sts).

Rounds 7–42: Work 1 sc in each sc.
Shape front

Round 43 (dec): Sc2tog, 1 sc in each of the next 32 sc, sc2tog (34 sts).

Round 44 (dec): Sc2tog, 1 sc in each of the next 30 sc, sc2tog (32 sts).

Round 45 (dec): Sc2tog, 1 sc in each of the next 28 sc, sc2tog (30 sts).

Round 46 (dec): Sc2tog, 1 sc in each of the next 26 sc, sc2tog (28 sts).

Round 47 (dec): Sc2tog, 1 sc in each of the next 24 sc, sc2tog (26 sts).

Round 48 (dec): Sc2tog, 1 sc in each of the next 22 sc, sc2tog (24 sts).

Neck

Rounds 49–51: Work 1 sc in each sc. Sl st to next st and fasten off.

Front legs (make 2)

Starting at the base of the paw, with C/2–D/3 hook and A, wind yarn around finger a couple of times to form a ring, insert the hook into the ring, catch the yarn and draw it back through the ring.

Round 1: 1 ch (does not count as a st), work 6 sc into ring (12 sts).

Round 2 (inc): (2 sc in next sc) 6 times (12 sts). Pull on short end of yarn to close ring.

Round 3 (inc): (2 sc in next sc, 1 sc) 6 times (18 sts).

Round 4: 1 sc in back loop only of each sc. This will help create a flat base.

Round 5: Work 1 sc in each sc.

Shape paw

Round 6 (dec): 1 sc in next 3 sc, (sc2tog) 6 times, 1 sc in next 3 sc (12 sts).

Rounds 7–12: Work 1 sc in each sc.

Shape leg

Round 13 (inc): (2 sc in next sc, 3 sc) 3 times (15 sts).

Round 14: Work 1 sc in each sc.

Round 15 (inc): (2 sc in next sc, 4 sc) 3 times (18 sts).

Round 16: Work 1 sc in each sc.

Round 17 (inc): (2 sc in next sc, 5 sc) 3 times (21 sts).

Round 18: Work 1 sc in each sc.

Round 19 (inc): (2 sc in next sc, 6 sc) 3 times (24 sts).

Round 20: Work 1 sc in each sc.
Sl st to next st and fasten off.

Hind legs (make 2)

Starting at the base of the paw, with C/2–D/3 hook and A, wind yarn around finger a couple of times to form a ring, insert the hook into the ring, catch the yarn and draw it back through the ring. Work rounds 1–6 as for front legs.

Rounds 7–10: Work 1 sc in each sc.

Shape leg

Round 11 (inc): 1 sc in next 5 sc, (2 sc in next sc) twice, 1 sc in next 5 sc (14 sts).

Round 12: Work 1 sc in each sc.

Round 13 (inc): 1 sc in next 6 sc, (2 sc in next sc) twice, 1 sc in next 6 sc (16 sts).

Round 14: Work 1 sc in each sc.

Round 15 (inc): 1 sc in next 7 sc, (2 sc in next sc) twice, 1 sc in next 7 sc (18 sts).

Round 16: Work 1 sc in each sc.

Round 17 (inc): 1 sc in next 8 sc, (2 sc in next sc) twice, 1 sc in next 8 sc (20 sts).

Round 18: Work 1 sc in each sc.

Round 19 (inc): 1 sc in next 9 sc, (2 sc in next sc) twice, 1 sc in next 9 sc (22 sts).

Round 20 (inc): 1 sc in next 10 sc, (2 sc in next sc) twice, 1 sc in next 10 sc (24 sts).

Round 21 (inc): 1 sc in next 11 sc, (2 sc in next sc) twice, 1 sc in next 11 sc (26 sts).
Sl st to next st and fasten off.

Front legs

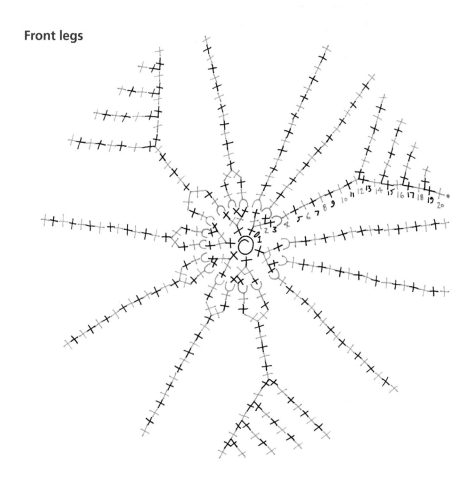

Hind legs

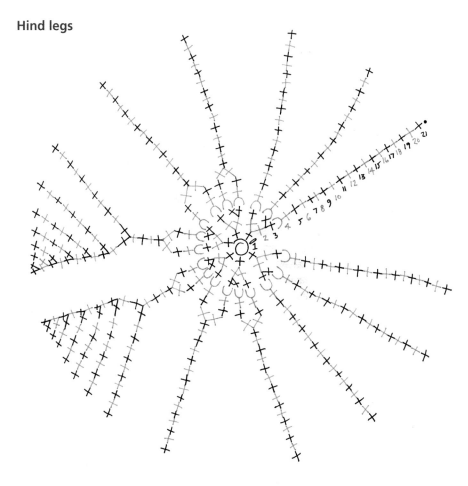

Ears

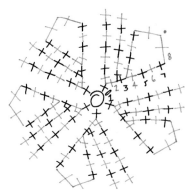

lion

Tail

JOIN STITCHES TO FORM A CORD

Ears (make 2)

Starting at the top of the ear, with C/2–D/3 hook and A, wind yarn around finger a couple of times to form a ring, insert the hook into the ring, catch the yarn and draw it back through the ring.

Round 1: 1 ch (does not count as a st), work 5 sc into ring (5 sts).

Round 2 (inc): (2 sc in next sc) 5 times. Pull on short end to close ring (10 sts).

Round 3 (inc): (2 sc in next sc, 1 sc) 5 times (15 sts).

Round 4 (inc): (2 sc in next sc, 2 sc) 5 times (20 sts).

Rounds 5–7: Work 1 sc in each sc.

Round 8 (dec): (Sc2tog, 2 sc) 5 times (15 sts).

Sl st to next st and fasten off, leaving a long length of yarn.

Tail

With C/2–D/3 hook and A, make 23 ch. 1 sc into second ch from hook, 1 sc into each of the next 21 ch (22 sts).

Next: 1 ch, sl st into both the back loop of the next sc and the reverse side of the ch at the same time to join and form a cord.

Tassel

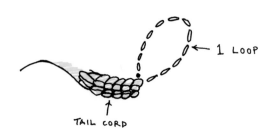

Nose

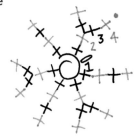

Mane

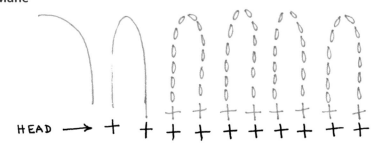

Tassel

With C/2–D/3 hook and A, (make 12 ch, sl st into the end of the cord to form a loop) 7 times (7 loops). Fasten off.

Nose

With B/1–C/2 hook and C, wind yarn around finger a few times to form a ring, insert the hook into the ring, catch the yarn and draw it back through the ring.

Round 1: 1 ch (does not count as a st), work 6 sc into ring (6 sts).

Round 2: Work 1 sc in each sc.

Round 3 (inc): (2 sc in next sc, 1 sc) 3 times (9 sts). Pull on short end to close ring.

Round 4: Work 1 sc in each sc.

Sl st to next st and fasten off, leaving a length of yarn at the end.

KINGS OF COOL
Their eyes are six times more sensitive to light than ours. That's why they are often photographed wearing sunglasses.

Finishing

Body
Stuff the body firmly, filling it right to the top of the neck opening. Sew the head in place with the longer shaping at the front of the face positioned vertically, so it is long rather than wide.

Legs
Stuff the legs firmly right up to the opening and keeping the base of the paws flat. Sew the legs in place, with the paws facing forward. Stitch all around each leg to hold them securely in place.

Ears
Flatten each ear and, with the long length of yarn left, sew each side together to join, forming a straight edge. Bring the two corners at the lower edge of the ear to the middle and stitch together to produce a bowl shape. Run a gathering stitch around the lower edge of the ear, draw up and secure with a few stitches before sewing in place to each side of the head.

Tail
Stitch the tail in place at the end of the lion.

Nose
Flatten the nose and, with the length of yarn left after fastening off, sew the stitches from each side to join, forming a straight edge. Neatly sew the nose to the face, aligning the straight edge with the last round of yarn B. With C doubled, work a French knot each side of the face for the eyes.

Mane
With C/2–D/3 hook and A, join the yarn under the chin into the 14th round of the head.

Next: Work 1 sc into the next st, make 12 ch and work 1 sc into the next st. This makes one 12 ch loop. Continue making the loops, working around the ears and covering every round to the back of the head and a little way down the neck and front shaping. The "fur" can be made fuller by adding a few more chain stitches to the loops. Finish by fluffing with fingers to style the mane.

The sunny yellow and chocolate shades used here can be replaced with cream and reddish-brown yarns if you'd like to give a more natural coloring to this jolly giraffe.

Giraffe

DID YOU KNOW?

Giraffes are born with horn-like structures called ossicones on their heads. If there are tufts of hair on top then the giraffe is probably female.

Information you'll need

Finished size
Approximately 11½in (29cm) tall (not including the ears)

Materials
Rico Design Essentials Merino DK (or equivalent DK weight yarn, CYCA 3), 100% merino wool (131yds/120m per 50g ball)
2 x 50g balls in 065 Yellow (A)
1 x 50g ball in 057 Chocolate (B)
B/1–C/2 (UK12:2.5mm) and C/2–D/3 (UK11:3mm) crochet hooks
Darning needle
Toy stuffing
Knitting needle or pencil to aid in stuffing giraffe
Air-erasable fabric marker or tailor's chalk pencil
Embroidery needle
Stranded embroidery thread in dark brown

Gauge
22 sts and 24 rounds to 4in (10cm) over single crochet using C/2–D/3 hook

Key

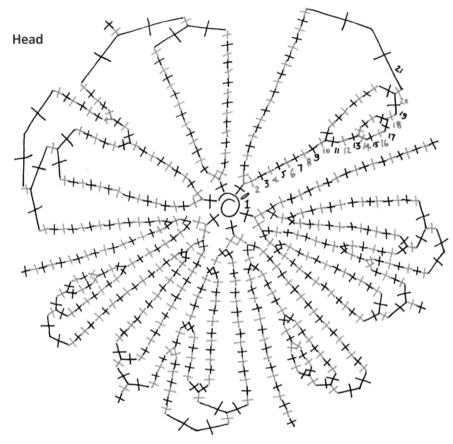

Head

◯ Wind yarn around finger to form a ring

• Slip stitch (sl st)

/ Chain (ch)

+ Single crochet (sc)

⋎⋏ 2 sc in same st

⋏⋏ sc2tog

⋎⋔⋏ 3 sc in same st

⊤ Single crochet into back loop only

⊍ Single crochet into back loop of both stitches at the same time to join

⌒ Slip stitch into back loop of single crochet and chain at the same time to join

How to make Giraffe

The pieces are all crocheted separately and stitched together. The head, body, legs, and ossicones (horns) are worked in continuous rounds. The front of the body is shaped by working in rows and decreasing the stitches at the center front. The ears are made in two pieces, worked in rows, and joined by crocheting them together. The tail is a crocheted cord with a small tassel added to the tip. Small crocheted squares form the markings, which are sewn over the back of the body and neck. Embroidered eyes and nostrils complete the giraffe.

Head

Starting at the tip of the nose, with C/2–D/3 hook and A, wind yarn around a finger a couple of times to form a ring, insert the hook, catch the yarn and draw back through the ring.

Round 1: 1 ch (does not count as a st), work 6 sc into ring (6 sts).

Round 2 (inc): (2 sc in same st) 6 times (12 sts). Pull on short end of yarn to close ring.

Round 3 (inc): 1 sc in each of next 6 sc, (2 sc in same st) 6 times (18 sts).

Round 4: Work 1 sc in each sc.

Round 5 (inc): 1 sc in each of next 6 sc, (2 sc in same st, 1 sc) 6 times (24 sts).

Rounds 6–10: Work 1 sc in each sc.

Round 11 (inc): (2 sc in same st, 3 sc) 6 times (30 sts).

Rounds 12–13: Work 1 sc in each sc.

Round 14 (inc): (2 sc in same st, 4 sc) 6 times (36 sts).

Rounds 15–16: Work 1 sc in each sc.

Shape back of head

Round 17 (dec): (Sc2tog, 2 sc) 9 times (27 sts).

Round 18: Work 1 sc in each sc.

Round 19 (dec): (Sc2tog, 1 sc) 9 times (18 sts).

Round 20: Work 1 sc in each sc.

Round 21 (dec): (Sc2tog, 1 sc) 6 times (12 sts).

Fasten off, leaving a length of yarn and thread through the last round of stitches. Stuff the head firmly, gather up the opening and stitch to secure.

Body
Rounds 1–23

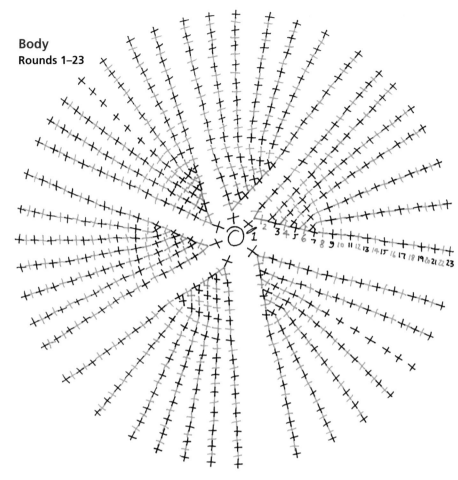

Shape front of body
Rows 1–9

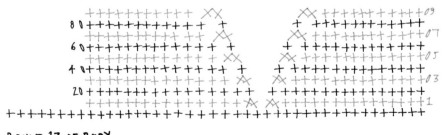

ROUND 23 OF BODY

Body

Starting at tail end, with C/2–D/3 hook and A, wind yarn around to form ring, insert hook, catch yarn, draw back through ring.

Round 1: 1 ch (does not count as a st), work 6 sc into ring (6 sts).

Round 2 (inc): (2 sc in same st) 6 times (12 sts). Pull on short end of yarn to close ring.

Round 3 (inc): (2 sc in same st, 1 sc) 6 times (18 sts).

Round 4 (inc): (2 sc in same st, 2 sc) 6 times (24 sts).

Round 5 (inc): (2 sc in same st, 3 sc) 6 times (30 sts).

Round 6 (inc): (2 sc in same st, 4 sc) 6 times (36 sts).

Round 7 (inc): (2 sc in same st, 5 sc) 6 times (42 sts).

Rounds 8–23: Work 1 sc in each sc.

Shape front

Row 1 (RS) (dec): Work 1 sc in next 15 sc, (sc2tog) twice, 1 sc in next 15 sc, turn.

Row 2: 1 ch (does not count as a st), 1 sc in next 32 sc, turn.

Row 3 (dec): 1 ch (does not count as a st), work 1 sc in next 14 sc, (sc2tog) twice, 1 sc in next 14 sc, turn.

Row 4: 1 ch (does not count as a st), 1 sc in next 30 sc, turn.

Row 5 (dec): 1 ch (does not count as a st), work 1 sc in next 13 sc, (sc2tog) twice, 1 sc in next 13 sc, turn.

Row 6: 1 ch (does not count as a st), 1 sc in next 28 sc, turn.

Row 7 (dec): 1 ch (does not count as a st), 1 sc in next 12 sc, (sc2tog) twice, 1 sc in next 12 sc, turn.

Row 8: 1 ch (does not count as a st), 1 sc in each 26 sc, turn.

Row 9 (dec): 1 ch (does not count as a st), 1 sc in next 11 sc, (sc2tog) twice, 1 sc in next 11 sc, turn.

Join center front

Row 10: With both sides together and right side facing, 1 ch, work 1 sc into the back loops only of each of the 12 sc from both sides at the same time to join. This will leave an opening at the top of the body for the neck shaping. Fasten off.

Shape neck

With right side facing, with C/2–D/3 hook and A, rejoin yarn to the center front of the opening at the top of the body.

Round 1: Work 1 sc in the stitches at the end of each of the 9 rows of the front shaping, 1 sc in each of the next 8 sc of the back, work 1 sc in the stitches at the opposite end of the 9 rows of the front shaping (26 sts).

Round 2 (dec): Sc2tog, 1 sc in next 22 sc, sc2tog (24 sts).

Round 3 (dec): (Sc2tog, 4 sc) 4 times (20 sts).

Rounds 4–14: Work 1 sc in each sc.

Round 15 (dec): (Sc2tog, 3 sc) 4 times (16 sts).

Rounds 16–21: Work 1 sc in each sc. Sl st to next st and fasten off.

Front legs (make 2)

Starting at the hoof, with C/2–D/3 hook and B, wind yarn around finger a couple of times to form a ring, insert the hook into the ring, catch the yarn and draw it back through the ring.

Round 1: 1 ch (does not count as a st), work 6 sc into ring (6 sts).

Round 2 (inc): (2 sc in same st) 6 times (12 sts). Pull on short end of yarn to close ring.

Round 3: 1 sc in back loop only of each sc. This will help create a flat base.

Rounds 4–6: Work 1 sc in each sc. Join and continue in A.

Rounds 7–32: Work 1 sc in each sc. Sl st to next st and fasten off.

Shape neck

Join center front

Front legs

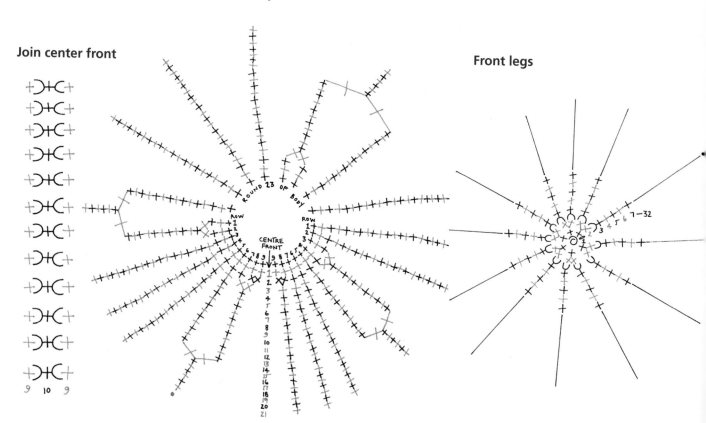

Hind legs (make 2)

Starting at the hoof, with C/2–D/3 hook and B, wind yarn around finger a couple of times to form a ring, insert the hook into the ring, catch the yarn and draw it back through the ring.

Work rounds 1–26 as for front legs.

Round 27 (inc): 2 sc in same st, 1 sc in next 10 sc, 2 sc in same st (14 sts).

Round 28: Work 1 sc in each sc.

Round 29 (inc): 2 sc in same st, 1 sc in next 12 sc, 2 sc in same st (16 sts).

Round 30: Work 1 sc in each sc.

Round 31 (inc): 2 sc in same st, 1 sc in next 14 sc, 2 sc in same st (18 sts).

Round 32: Work 1 sc in each sc.

Shape top of leg

Round 33 (inc): (2 sc in same st) twice, 1 sc in next 5 sc, (sc2tog) twice, 1 sc in next 5 sc, (2 sc in same st) twice (20 sts).

Round 34: Work 1 sc in each sc.

Round 35 (inc): (2 sc in same st) twice, 1 sc in next 6 sc, (sc2tog) twice, 1 sc in next 6 sc, (2 sc in same st) twice (22 sts).

Round 36: Work 1 sc in each sc.

Round 37 (inc): (2 sc in same st) twice, 1 sc in next 7 sc, (sc2tog) twice, 1 sc in next 7 sc, (2 sc in same st) twice (24 sts).

Sl st to next st and fasten off.

Hind legs
Rounds 1–26

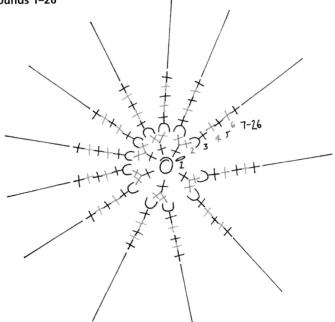

Hind legs
Rounds 26–37

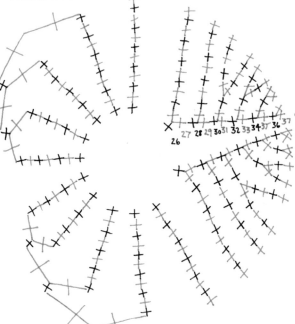

giraffe

Ears

Join ear pieces

STEPPING OUT

Every stride a giraffe takes is 15ft (4.6m) long so you'll end up very tired if you go for a stroll with one.

Outer ears (make 2)

With C/2–D/3 hook and A, make 9 ch.
Row 1 (RS): 1 sc in second ch from hook, 1 sc in next 6 ch, 3 sc in next ch, 1 sc into each of reverse side of ch, turn (17 sts).
Row 2 (inc): 1 ch (does not count as a st), 1 sc in next 8 sc, 3 sc in next sc, 1 sc in next 8 sc, turn (19 sts).
Row 3 (inc): 1 ch (does not count as a st), 1 sc in next 9 sc, 3 sc in next sc, 1 sc in next 9 sc (21 sts).
Fasten off.

Inner ears (make 2)

With C/2–D/3 hook and B, make 9 ch.
Work rows 1–3 as for outer ears.
Fasten off.

Join ear pieces

Place the wrong sides of the ear pieces together with the inner piece facing you. Using C/2–D/3 hook and yarn A, join the inner and outer ear pieces by working 1 sc in each sc of both ear pieces at the same time, inserting the hook under both loops of each stitch. Fasten off, leaving a long length of yarn. Weave in the short ends.

Ossicones

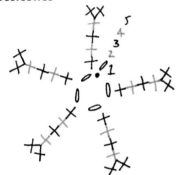

Tail

JOIN STITCHES TO FORM A CORD

Ossicones (make 2)

The horn-like protrusions on the head are crocheted using B/1–C/2 hook and A. Leaving a long length of yarn at the beginning, make 4 ch and join with a sl st to the first ch to form a ring.

Round 1: 1 ch (does not count as a st), work 5 sc into ring (5 sts).

Round 2: Work 1 sc in each sc. Use the end of a pencil to push the work to the right side as it has a tendency to curl inside out.

Rounds 3–4: Work 1 sc in each sc.

Round 5: Join B, (2 sc in same st) 5 times (10 sts).

Fasten off yarn and thread through a blunt-ended darning needle. Work a running stitch in and out of the back loops of the 10 sts, draw up to close and fasten off.

Tail

With C/2–D/3 hook and A, make 16 ch. 1 sc into second ch from hook, 1 sc into each of the next 14 ch, turn (15 sts).

Next: 1 ch, sl st into both the back loop of the next sc and the reverse side of the ch at the same time to join and form a cord. Fasten off, leaving a long length of yarn. Weave in the short end.

Markings

Markings (make 16)

With C/2–D/3 hook and B, make 4 ch and join with a sl st to the first ch to form a ring.

Round 1: 1 ch (does not count as a st), work 8 sc into ring (8 sts).

Round 2 (inc): *(1 sc, 2 ch, 1 sc) in next sc, 1 sc in next sc; rep from * a further 3 times, sl st to first sc and fasten off, leaving a long length of yarn.

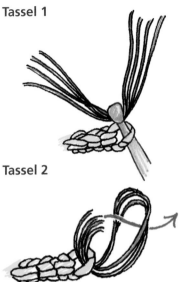

Tassel 1

Tassel 2

Finishing

Body
Stuff the body firmly, filling it right to the top of the neck opening. Use a knitting needle or the end of a pencil to push the stuffing to the end of the body. Sew the head in place with the sloped shaping positioned so it is under the chin, with the flatter side at the top.

Legs
Stuff the legs firmly, filling them right up to the opening and keeping the base of the hooves flat. Stitch the front legs side by side, just a few rows back from the front of the body. Sew the hind legs next to each other with the bend in the leg facing toward the back. Stitch all around each leg to hold them securely in place.

Ears
With the long length of yarn left, sew the lower edges of the inner and outer ear pieces together to join. Bring the two corners at each side of the lower edge of the ear to the middle and stitch together to shape, with the inner piece on the inside. Run a gathering stitch around the lower edge of the ear, draw up and secure with a few stitches before sewing in place to each side of the head.

Ossicones
Use the end of the crochet hook to push a tiny amount of stuffing into the ossicones to help keep them upright and sew them onto the head in between the ears.

Tail
To make the tasseled end of the tail, cut four 4in (10cm) lengths of yarn B and fold the lengths in half to form a loop. Insert the crochet hook into the end of the tail and catch the looped yarn (see 1). Pull the loop a little way through, remove the hook and then thread the ends back through the loop, pulling them tight (see 2). Trim the ends and sew the tail in place at the end of the giraffe.

Markings
Sew the markings on the back and neck of the giraffe.

Head
Use an air-erasable fabric marker or a tailor's chalk pencil to lightly mark the outline of the eyes and the nostrils. With four strands of brown embroidery thread, embroider the curved eye line in chain stitch and five eyelashes in straight stitch. Embroider the nostrils in satin stitch, working just two or three stitches for each one.

The pattern that forms the feathery design on the body of this retro-style owl looks complicated but is in fact simple to make and is very effective.

Owl

Information you'll need

Finished size
Approximately 9in (23cm) high x 7½in (19cm) at the widest part

Materials
Bergère de France Baronval (or equivalent DK weight yarn, CYCA 3), 60% wool, 40% acrylic (137yds/125m per 50g ball)
1 x 50g ball in 21376 Bizet (A)
1 x 50g ball in 25140 Plomb (B)
1 x 50g ball in 23118 Havane (C)
Scrap of DK yarn in black (D)
Bergère de France Lavandou (or equivalent DK weight yarn, CYCA 3), 59% acrylic, 30% cotton, 11% polyester (142 yds/130m per 50g ball)
1 x 50g ball in 28951 Calisson (E)
C/2–D/3 (UK11:3mm) and E/4 (UK9:3.5mm) crochet hooks
Toy stuffing
Darning needle

Gauge
21 sts and 21 rounds to 4in (10cm) over single crochet using C/2–D/3 hook

Key

- ✐ Chain (ch)
- • Slip stitch (sl st)
- + Single crochet (sc)
- XX 2 sc in same st
- XX sc2tog
- ⊥̆ Single crochet into front loop only
- ∩̆ Single crochet into back loop only
- ⊤ Double (dc)
- ⋎ 2 dc in same st

Head

Starting at the top of the head, with C/2–D/3 hook and A, make 37 ch.

Round 1: 1 sc in second ch from hook, 1 sc in each of the next 34 ch, 2 sc into the next ch, 1 sc into the reverse side of each ch to the end (72 sts).

Rounds 2–21: Work 1 sc in each sc.

Round 22: Work 1 sc into front loops only of each sc.

Round 23: Work 1 sc in both loops of each sc.

Scalloped edge

Round 24: (1 sc in next sc, sk next sc, 5 dc in next sc, sk next sc) 18 times, sl st to next st and fasten off (18 scallops).

Head
Rounds 1–24

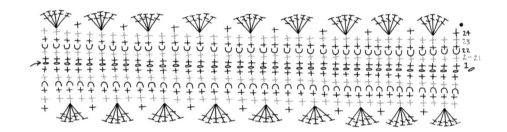

How to make Owl

The body is crocheted in one piece in rounds, starting with a length of chain stitches. A scalloped edge is crocheted in to separate the head from the feathery body, which is formed by a pattern of five doubles worked into one stitch and a single crochet in the next. The wings are semicircular in shape, worked in rows of single crochet. The eyes are made from rounds of double and chain stitches; the beak is worked in rounds of single crochet, which is then folded and stuffed before being attached to the face. The cone-shaped feet are formed in rounds of single crochet. After stuffing them, two rows of back stitch are worked through all the layers to create the shaping.

Feathers

With C/2–D/3 hook and B, join yarn to the back loop of the first sc on round 21.

Round 1: 1 sc into back loops only of each sc of round 21 (72 sts).

Round 2: Work 1 sc into both loops of each sc.

Round 3: (1 sc in next sc, sk next 2 sc, 5 dc in next sc, sk next 2 sc) 12 times, sl st to first sc (12 scallops).

Round 4: 3 ch (to count as first dc), 4 dc in first sc, (1 sc into third of 5 dc, 5 dc in next sc) 11 times, 1 sc into third of 5 dc, sl st to third of 3 ch (12 scallops).

Round 5: Sl st into next dc, 1 sc into next dc, (5 dc into next sc, 1 sc into third of 5 dc) 11 times, 5 dc into next sc, sl st to first sc.

Rounds 6–11: Rep rounds 4–5 a further 3 times.

Round 12: 1 ch (to count as first sc), work 1 sc into each stitch (72 sts).

Round 13: Work 1 sc in each sc.

Shape body

Round 14 (dec): (Sc2tog, 6 sc) 9 times (63 sts).

Round 15: Work 1 sc in each sc.

Round 16 (dec): (Sc2tog, 5 sc) 9 times (54 sts).

Round 17: Work 1 sc in each sc.

Shape base

Round 18 (dec): (Sc2tog, 4 sc) 9 times (45 sts).

Round 19 (dec): (Sc2tog, 3 sc) 9 times (36 sts).

Round 20 (dec): (Sc2tog, 2 sc) 9 times (27 sts).

Round 21 (dec): (Sc2tog, 1 sc) 9 times (18 sts).

Sl st to next st and fasten off, leaving a long length of yarn.

Feathers

Rounds 1–13,
Rounds 6, 8 and
10 as round 4
Rounds 7, 9
and 11 as
round 5

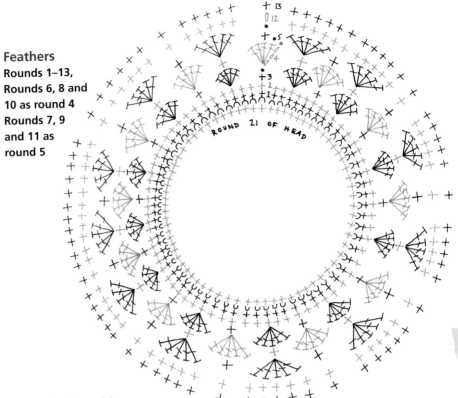

Shape body and base
Rounds 13–21

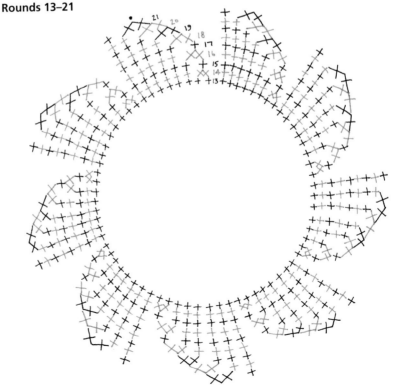

Wings

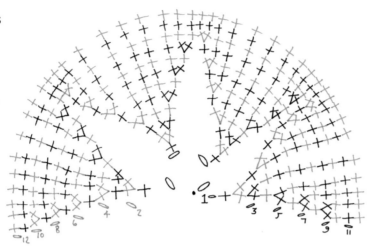

Wings (make 2)

With E/4 hook and C, make 4 ch and sl st to the first ch to form a ring.

Row 1: 1 ch (does not count as a st), work 4 sc into ring, turn (4 sts).

Row 2 (inc): 1 ch (does not count as a st), (2 sc in same st) 4 times, turn (8 sts).

Row 3 (inc): 1 ch (does not count as a st), (2 sc in same st, 1 sc) 4 times, turn (12 sts).

Row 4 (inc): 1 ch (does not count as a st), (2 sc in same st, 2 sc) 4 times, turn (16 sts).

Row 5 (inc): 1 ch (does not count as a st), (2 sc in same st, 3 sc) 4 times, turn (20 sts).

Row 6 (inc): 1 ch (does not count as a st), (2 sc in same st, 4 sc) 4 times, turn (24 sts).

Row 7 (inc): 1 ch (does not count as a st), (2 sc in same st, 5 sc) 4 times, turn (28 sts).

Row 8 (inc): 1 ch (does not count as a st), (2 sc in same st, 6 sc) 4 times, turn (32 sts).

Row 9 (inc): 1 ch (does not count as a st), (2 sc in same st, 7 sc) 4 times, turn (36 sts).

Row 10 (inc): 1 ch (does not count as a st), (2 sc in same st, 8 sc) 4 times, turn (40 sts).

Rows 11–12 (inc): 1 ch (does not count as a st), 1 sc in each sc.

Fasten off, leaving length of yarn at end.

Eyes (make 2)

With C/2–D/3 hook and D, make 5 ch and join with a sl st to form a ring.

Round 1: 3 ch (counts as first dc), 13 dc into ring, sl st to third of 3 ch (14 sts). Join and continue in E.

Round 2 (inc): 3 ch (counts as first dc), 1 dc in first dc, (2 dc in same st) 13 times, sl st to third of 3 ch (28 sts).

Round 3 (inc): 4 ch (counts as first dc and 1 ch), (1 dc, 1 ch) into each of the next 27 dc, sl st to third of 4 ch (56 sts).

Round 4 (inc): 1 ch (does not count as a st), (2 sc into next 1 ch sp) 28 times, sl st to first sc and fasten off, leaving a long length of yarn.

Eyes

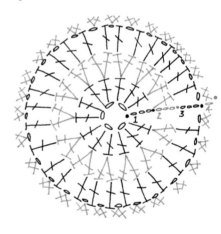

Feet

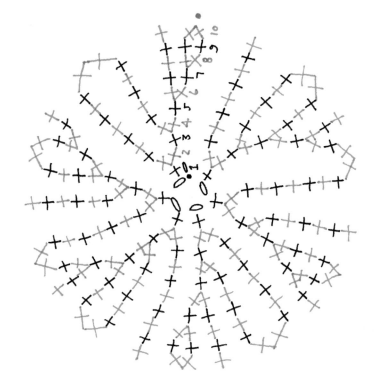

Beak

Beak

With C/2–D/3 hook and C, make 4 ch and join with a sl st to first ch to form a ring.
Round 1: 1 ch (does not count as a st), work 6 sc into ring (6 sts).
Round 2 (inc): (2 sc in same st) 6 times (12 sts).
Round 3 (inc): (2 sc in same st, 1 sc) 6 times (18 sts).
Round 4 (inc): (2 sc in same st, 2 sc) 6 times (24 sts).
Sl st to next st and fasten off, leaving a long length of yarn.

Feet (make 2)

With C/2–D/3 hook and C, make 4 ch and join with a sl st to first ch to form a ring.
Round 1: 1 ch (does not count as a st), work 6 sc into ring (6 sts).
Round 2 (inc): (2 sc in same st) 6 times (12 sts).
Round 3: Work 1 sc in each sc.
Round 4 (inc): (2 sc in same st, 1 sc) 6 times (18 sts).
Round 5: Work 1 sc in each sc.
Round 6 (inc): (2 sc in same st, 2 sc) 6 times (24 sts).

Round 7: Work 1 sc in each sc.
Round 8 (inc): (2 sc in same st, 3 sc) 6 times (30 sts).
Round 9: Work 1 sc in each sc.
Round 10 (dec): (Sc2tog, 1 sc) 10 times (20 sts).
Sl st to next st and fasten off.

owl

Finishing

Head and body

Push the stuffing right into the corners at the top of the head before filling the rest of the body so it is firmly stuffed. Thread the length of yarn left at the end onto a blunt-ended darning needle and weave through the last round of stitches, draw up to close the opening and fasten off. Weave in the ends. Flatten the base of the owl so it can sit easily on its own.

Wings

Use the length of yarn left after fastening off the wings to sew the straight edge of each one to the sides of the owl's body, stitching them down to the first round in yarn B so the joins are hidden beneath the scalloped edging of the head.

Eyes

Sew the eyes to the face just above the scalloped edge.

Feet

To finish each foot, bring the open edge of the last round to meet and sew the 10 stitches from both sides together to join, leaving a small opening to push some stuffing in before sewing it up. Weave in the ends. With the same shade of yarn, work two lines of back stitch through all the layers and over each round of crochet, starting from the heel and finishing at the wide front end to form a quilted effect that defines the shaping. Sew the feet to the base of the owl so they peep out from under the feathery body.

Beak

Fold the circular piece crocheted for the beak in half. With the length of yarn left after fastening off, sew the curved edges together, leaving a small opening to push a little stuffing through to fill the beak before closing. Stitch the beak in place in between the eyes with the curved side facing out, sewing all around it to secure it in position.

WHAT A HOOT

Unless they are hunting or feeding their young, owls are content just to take things easy.

owl

109

Any combination of greens can be used to create this agile frog.
Worked entirely in continuous rounds of single crochet, it makes
a nice, bright, and simple project.

Frog

frog

DID YOU KNOW?
Frogs are amphibians—they begin their lives in water as eggs and then tadpoles, then when they are fully developed they live mainly on land.

Information you'll need

Finished size
Body measures approximately 5in (12.5cm) in diameter; total length approximately 14in (35.5cm)

Materials
Adriafil Regina (or equivalent DK weight yarn, CYCA 3), 100% merino wool (137yds/125m per 50g ball)
3 x 50g balls in 098 Green/Yellow (A)
1 x 50g ball in 040 Light Green (B)
1 x 50g ball in 011 Cream (C)
Scrap of DK yarn in black
C/2–D/3 (UK11:3mm) crochet hook
Darning needle
Toy stuffing

Gauge
24 sts and 28 rounds to 4in (10cm) over single crochet using C/2–D/3 hook

Key

⌒ Chain (ch)

• Slip stitch (sl st)

✛ Single crochet (sc)

✕✕ 2 sc in same st

How to make Frog

The body is made in two halves, worked in continuous rounds of single crochet, forming a bowl shape that is joined by crocheting a round of stitches into both of them at the same time. The stitches create a ridge that forms the mouth of the frog. The eyes are made in the same way, with the ridge forming the edge of the eyelid. The legs are worked in continuous rounds to create a cone shape. Two cones make up each leg with the feet and toes attached. The arms are simple tubes, shaped at the hand, with the fingers stitched on. The limbs are attached to the body securely but keeping them pliable.

Body

Lower half

Starting at the center of the lower half of the body, with C/2–D/3 hook and B, make 4 ch and join with a sl st to the first ch to form a ring.

Round 1: 1 ch (does not count as a st), work 6 sc into ring (6 sts).

Round 2 (inc): (2 sc in same st) 6 times (12 sts).

Round 3 (inc): (2 sc in same st, 1 sc) 6 times (18 sts).

Round 4 (inc): (2 sc in same st, 2 sc) 6 times (24 sts).

Round 5 (inc): (2 sc in same st, 3 sc) 6 times (30 sts).

Round 6 (inc): (2 sc in same st, 4 sc) 6 times (36 sts).

Round 7 (inc): (2 sc in same st, 5 sc) 6 times (42 sts).

Round 8 (inc): (2 sc in same st, 6 sc) 6 times (48 sts).

Round 9 (inc): (2 sc in same st, 7 sc) 6 times (54 sts).

Round 10: Work 1 sc in each sc.

Round 11 (inc): (2 sc in same st, 8 sc) 6 times (60 sts).

Round 12: Work 1 sc in each sc.

Round 13 (inc): (2 sc in same st, 9 sc) 6 times (66 sts).

Round 14: Work 1 sc in each sc.

Round 15 (inc): (2 sc in same st, 10 sc) 6 times (72 sts).

Rounds 16–20: Work 1 sc in each sc. Sl st to next st and fasten off.

Upper half

With C/2–D/3 hook and A, make 4 ch and join with a sl st to the first ch to form a ring.

Work rounds 1–20 as for the lower half. Sl st to next st and fasten off.

Join the two halves

Join yarn A to the end of the last round on the lower half crocheted in B. With C/2–D/3 hook and A, place the wrong sides (the insides) of each piece together, matching the stitches. Insert the hook under both loops of the first sc of the lower half and then under both loops of the first sc of the upper half and work 1 sc to join the two stitches. Continue in this way, working together each of the sc from both pieces at the same time, being sure to insert the hook into a single crochet of the lower half first and then the upper half. This will create a ridge that lays toward the

bottom half, forming the frog's mouth. Leave a small opening to stuff the body firmly before continuing to join the remaining stitches of the 72 sc on both pieces as before. Sl st to next st and fasten off. Weave in the ends.

Eyes (make 2)
Eyeballs
With C/2–D/3 hook and C, make 4 ch and join with a sl st to the first ch to form a ring.
Round 1: 1 ch (does not count as a st), work 6 sc into ring (6 sts).
Round 2 (inc): (2 sc in same st) 6 times (12 sts).
Round 3 (inc): (2 sc in same st, 1 sc) 6 times (18 sts).
Round 4 (inc): (2 sc in same st, 2 sc) 6 times (24 sts).
Round 5: Work 1 sc in each sc.
Round 6 (inc): (2 sc in same st, 3 sc) 6 times (30 sts).
Round 7: Work 1 sc in each sc.
Sl st to next st and fasten off.

Eyeballs and eye sockets

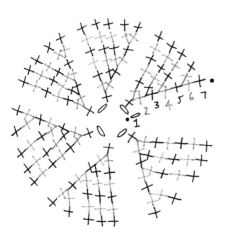

Body

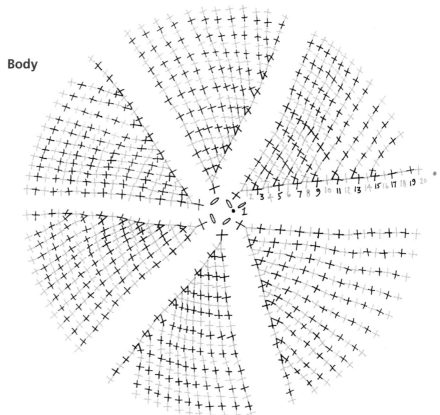

frog

Body
Join the two halves

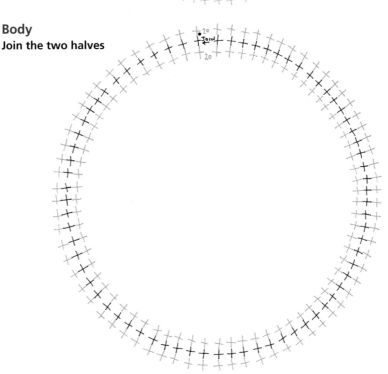

113

Eye sockets

With C/2–D/3 hook and A, make 4 ch and join with a sl st to the first ch to form a ring. Work rounds 1–7 as for the eyeballs. Sl st to next st and fasten off.

Join eye pieces

Join yarn A to the end of the last round on the eyeball. With C/2–D/3 hook and A, place the wrong sides (the insides) of each piece together, matching the stitches. Insert the hook under both loops of the first sc of the eyeball and then under both loops of the first sc of the eyelid and work 1 sc to join the two stitches. Continue in this way, working together each of the sc from both pieces at the same time,

inserting the hook into a single crochet of the eyeball first and then the eyelid. This creates a ridge that gives the impression that the eyelid encases the eye. Leave a small opening to stuff the piece before continuing to join the remaining stitches of the 30 sc on both pieces as before. Sl st to next st and fasten off, leaving a long length of yarn. Weave in the short ends.

Pupils

With C/2–D/3 hook and black DK yarn, make 4 ch and join with a sl st to the first ch to form a ring.

Next: 1 ch (does not count as a st), work 6 sc into ring (6 sts) Sl st to next st and fasten off, leaving a long length of yarn.

Arms (make 2)

With C/2–D/3 hook and A, make 4 ch and join with a sl st to the first ch to form a ring.

Round 1: 1 ch (does not count as a st), work 5 sc into ring (5 sts).

Round 2 (inc): (2 sc in same st) 5 times (10 sts).

Rounds 3–15: Work 1 sc in each sc.

Round 16 (inc): (2 sc in same st, 1 sc) 5 times (15 sts).

Round 17: Work 1 sc in each sc.

Round 18 (inc): (2 sc in same st, 2 sc) 5 times (20 sts).

Round 19: Work 1 sc in each sc.

Round 20 (inc): (2 sc in same st, 3 sc) 5 times (25 sts).

Join eye pieces

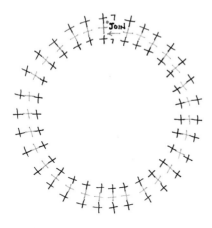

Arms

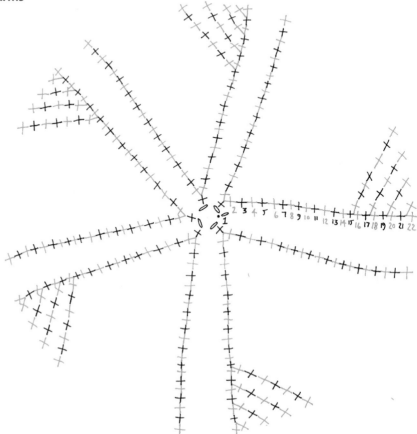

Pupils

Round 21: Work 1 sc in each sc.
Round 22 (inc): (2 sc in same st, 4 sc) 5 times (30 sts). Sl st to next st and fasten off, leaving length of yarn at the end.

Fingers (make 6)

With C/2–D/3 hook and A, make 4 ch and join with a sl st to the first ch to form a ring.
Round 1: 1 ch (does not count as a st), work 5 sc into ring (5 sts).
Round 2 (inc): (2 sc in same st) 5 times (10 sts).
Rounds 3–9: Work 1 sc in each sc. Sl st to next st and fasten off, leaving a long length of yarn at the end.

Legs (make 2)

With C/2–D/3 hook and A, make 4 ch and join with a sl st to the first ch to form a ring.
Round 1: 1 ch (does not count as a st), work 6 sc into ring (6 sts).
Round 2 (inc): (2 sc in same st) 6 times (12 sts).
Rounds 3–5: Work 1 sc in each sc.
Round 6 (inc): (2 sc in same st, 1 sc) 6 times (18 sts).
Rounds 7–9: Work 1 sc in each sc.
Round 10 (inc): (2 sc in same st, 2 sc) 6 times (24 sts).
Rounds 11–13: Work 1 sc in each sc.

Round 14 (inc): (2 sc in same st, 3 sc) 6 times (30 sts).
Rounds 15–17: Work 1 sc in each sc.
Round 18 (inc): (2 sc in same st, 4 sc) 6 times (36 sts).
Round 19–21: Work 1 sc in each sc.
Round 22 (inc): (2 sc in same st, 5 sc) 6 times (42 sts).
Rounds 23–25: Work 1 sc in each sc. Sl st to next st and fasten off, leaving a long length of yarn. Make one more piece for the same leg.

DID YOU KNOW?

Mother frogs lay thousands of eggs at one time, so frogs have big family reunions.

Fingers

Legs

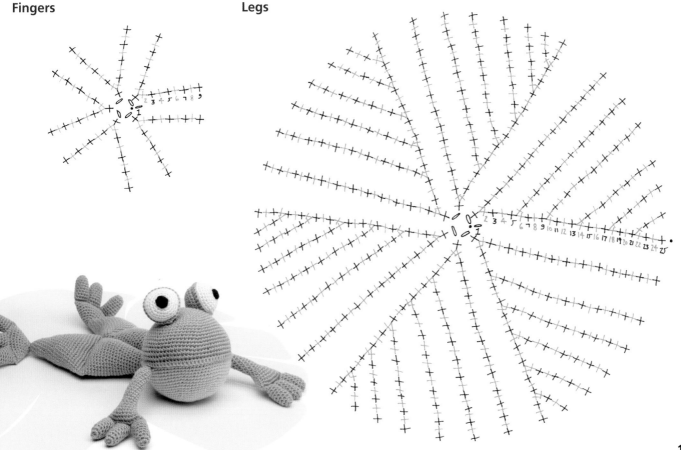

115

Feet (make 2)

With C/2–D/3 hook and A, make 4 ch and join with a sl st to the first ch to form a ring.

Round 1: 1 ch (does not count as a st), work 6 sc into ring (6 sts).

Round 2 (inc): (2 sc in same st) 6 times (12 sts).

Round 3: Work 1 sc in each sc.

Round 4 (inc): (2 sc in same st, 1 sc) 6 times (18 sts).

Round 5: Work 1 sc in each sc.

Round 6 (inc): (2 sc in same st, 2 sc) 6 times (24 sts).

Round 7: Work 1 sc in each sc.

Round 8 (inc): (2 sc in same st, 3 sc) 6 times (30 sts).

Round 9: Work 1 sc in each sc.

Round 10 (inc): (2 sc in same st, 4 sc) 6 times (36 sts).

Sl st to next st and fasten off, leaving a long length of yarn at the end.

Toes (make 6)

With C/2–D/3 hook and A, make 4 ch and join with a sl st to the first ch to form a ring.

Round 1: 1 ch (does not count as a st), work 6 sc into ring (6 sts).

Round 2 (inc): (2 sc in same st) 6 times (12 sts).

Rounds 3–10: Work 1 sc in each sc.

Sl st to next st and fasten off, leaving a long length of yarn at the end.

Feet

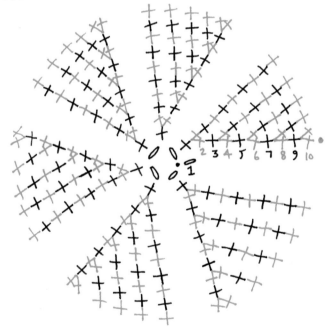

Toes

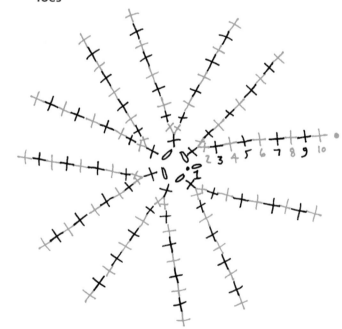

Finishing

Eyes

Use the length of yarn left after fastening off the pupils to sew them neatly to the center of each eyeball. Sew the eyes to the top of the head, stitching all around to hold them firmly in place.

Legs and arms

Stuff the leg pieces, pushing the stuffing firmly into the end, but filling it less near the opening so when the pieces are joined the leg can bend easily. Stuff the arms, fingers, feet, and toes. Squeeze the open end of each piece together and use the lengths of yarn left after fastening off to sew the stitches from each side together to form a straight edge. Stitch the straight end of three fingers to the straight edge of

each arm and sew three toes to each foot in the same way. Sew the straight seams of each leg piece together to form the knee joint. Stitch each foot to one end of each leg, sewing it securely but still allowing movement. Sew the other end of each leg together to join them before stitching them at the join to the center of the back of the frog's body, positioning them just under the ridge and stitching them so they are securely in place but can still move about. The legs should fall loosely when the frog is picked up and can be bent at each side of the frog when in a sitting position. Sew the arms to each side of the body, just under the ridge that forms the mouth. Weave in the ends.

SPRING TIME
Some frogs can jump up to 20 times their own body length in a single leap. Wheeeeeeee!

frog

If you are substituting another yarn for this beautiful bird project, choose cotton instead of wool, as it is heavier so the feathers will hang much better.

Flamingo

Information you'll need

Finished size
Approximately 30½in (77.5cm) high

Materials
Sirdar Calico DK (or equivalent DK weight yarn, CYCA 3), 60% cotton, 40% acrylic (172yds/158m per 50g ball)
2 x 50g balls in 735 Shrimp (A)
Scraps of any DK yarn in black (B) and white (C)
Sirdar Snuggly Smiley Stripes DK (or equivalent DK weight yarn, CYCA 3), 80% bamboo (sourced viscose), 20% wool (104yds/95m per 50g ball) or any multi-colored DK yarn
1 x 50g ball in 259 Mini Haha (D)
Patons 100% Cotton 4ply (or equivalent DK weight yarn, CYCA 3), 100% cotton (361yds/330m per 100g ball)
1 x 100g ball in 1725 Pink (E)
B/1–C/2 (UK12:2.5mm), C/2–D/3 (UK11:3mm), and E/4 (UK9:3.5mm) crochet hooks
Darning needle
Toy stuffing
Knitting needle or pencil to aid in stuffing
Embroidery needle
Safety pins

Gauge
22 sts and 22 rows to 4in (10cm) over single crochet using C/2–D/3 hook

MIRROR MIRROR
Flamingos spend 15 to 30 percent of the day preening. But you'd do that if you were that pretty too.

flamingo

Key

- Wind yarn around finger to form a ring
- Slip stitch (sl st)
- Chain (ch)
- Single crochet (sc)
- Single crochet into back loop only
- 2 sc in same st
- sc2tog
- Half double crochet (hdc)
- 2 hdc in next st
- Double crochet (dc)
- Treble (tr)
- Double treble (dtr)
- Double crochet around post of stitch
- Treble around post of stitch
- Double treble around post of stitch

Head
Rounds 1–15

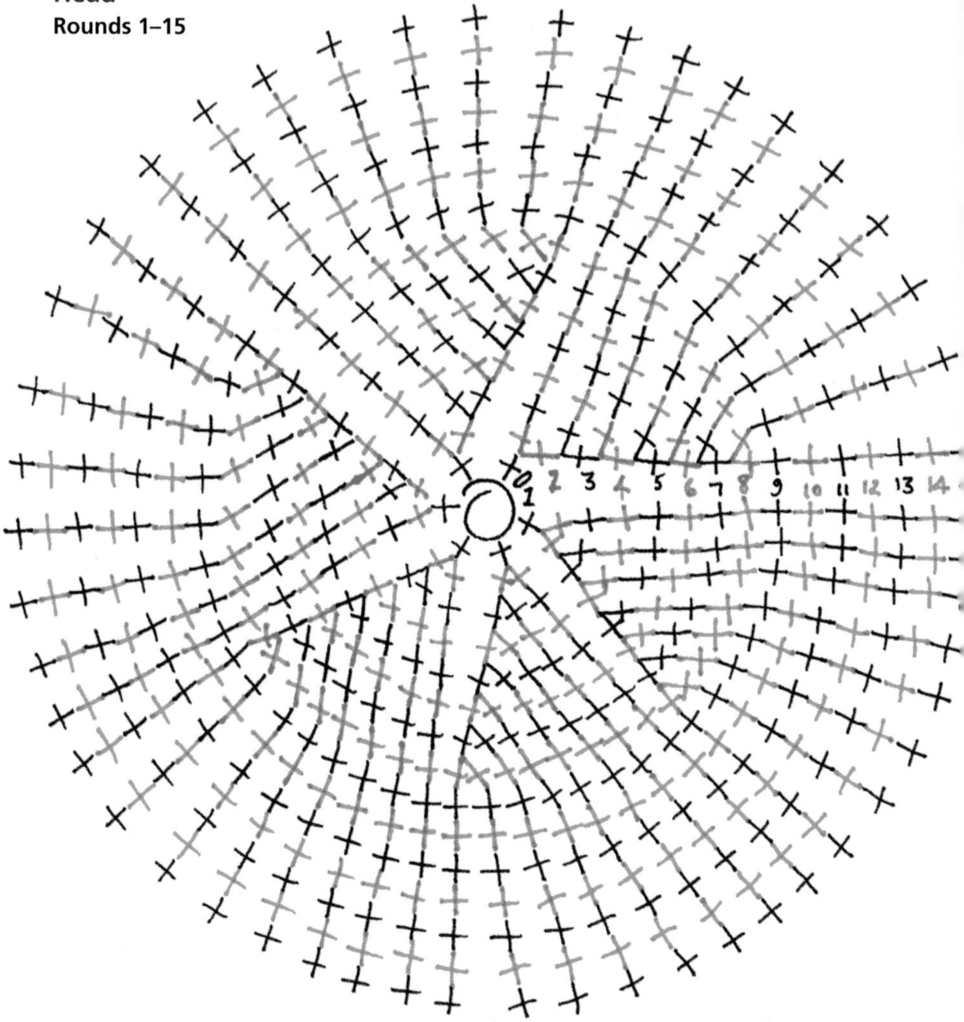

How to make Flamingo

The head and body are crocheted in one piece in a combination of rounds and rows. The beak and eyes are worked separately. The feathers are formed by crocheting a foundation of double crochet stitches and then working the next row around the posts of the doubles, rather than into the tops of the stitches as normal. The legs are made in two pieces worked in continuous rounds. The open ends are sewn flat and joined so they can bend at the knee and body. The feet are made in continuous rounds that are then divided into three to form the toes and then stuffed and handstitched through the layers to enhance the shaping.

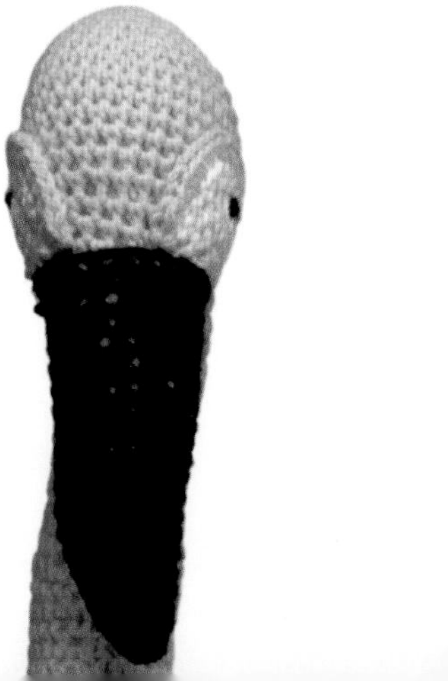

Divide for beak

Shape neck
Rows 1–40

ROUND 15 →
OF HEAD

ROW 1

flamingo

Head
Start at top of head, with C/2–D/3 hook and A, wind yarn to form ring, insert hook, catch yarn and draw back through ring.

Round 1: Make 1 ch (does not count as st), 6 sc into ring (6 sts).

Round 2 (inc): (2 sc in same st) 6 times, pull on short end to close ring (12 sts).

Round 3 (inc): (2 sc in next sc, 1 sc) 6 times (18 sts).

Round 4 (inc): (2 sc in next sc, 2 sc) 6 times (24 sts).

Round 5 (inc): (2 sc in next sc, 3 sc) 6 times (30 sts).

Round 6 (inc): (2 sc in next sc, 4 sc) 6 times (36 sts).

Round 7 (inc): (2 sc in next sc, 5 sc) 6 times (42 sts).

Round 8 (inc): (2 sc in next sc, 6 sc) 6 times (48 sts).

Rounds 9–15: Work 1 sc in each sc.

Divide for beak
Round 16: 1 sc in next 12 sc, turn and work 1 sc in the opposite 12 sc to form the shaping. Sl st to next st and fasten off.

Shape neck
With beak shaping on RHS of work, rejoin yarn A and cont on rem 24 sc for the neck.

Row 1: 1 sc in next 24 sc, turn.

Rows 2–3: 1 ch (does not count as a st), 1 sc in each sc, turn.

Row 4: 1 ch (does not count as a st), 2 sc in same st, 9 sc, (sc2tog) twice, 9 sc, 2 sc in same st, turn.

Row 5: 1 ch (does not count as a st), work 1 sc in each sc, turn.

Row 6: As row 4.

Row 7: 1 ch (does not count as a st), work 1 sc in each sc, turn.

Row 8: 1 ch (does not count as a st), (2 sc in next sc) twice, 6 sc, (sc2tog) 4 times, 6 sc, (2 sc in next sc) twice, turn.

Rows 9–24: Rep last 2 rows 8 times.

Rows 25–27: 1 ch (does not count as st), work 1 sc in each sc, turn.

Row 28 (inc): 1 ch (does not count as st), 2 sc in next sc, 22 sc, 2 sc in next sc (26 sts).

Rows 29–34: 1 ch (does not count as a st), work 1 sc in each sc, turn.

Row 35 (inc): 1 ch (does not count as a st), 8 sc, (2 sc in next sc, 2 sc) 4 times, 6 sc, turn (30 sts).

Row 36 (inc): 1 ch (does not count as a st), 13 sc, (2 sc in next sc) 4 times, 13 sc, turn (34 sts).

Row 37 (inc): 1 ch (does not count as a st), 15 sc, (2 sc in next sc) 4 times, 15 sc, turn (38 sts).

Row 38 (inc): 1 ch (does not count as st), 17 sc, (2 sc in next sc) 4 times, 17 sc, turn (42 sts).

Row 39 (inc): 1 ch (does not count as st), 6 sc, (2 sc in next sc, 1 sc) 15 times, 6 sc, turn (57 sts).

Row 40: 1 ch (does not count as a st), work 1 sc in each sc, turn.

Row 41 (inc): 1 ch (does not count as a st), 7 sc, (2 sc in next sc, 2 sc) 14 times, 2 sc in next sc, 7 sc, turn (72 sts).

Row 42: 1 ch (does not count as a st),

work 1 sc in each sc, turn.

Row 43: 1 ch (does not count as a st), (sc2tog) twice, 30 sc, (2 sc in next sc) 4 times, 30 sc, (sc2tog) twice, turn.

Row 44: 1 ch (does not count as a st), work 1 sc in each sc, turn.

Rows 45–52: Repeat the last 2 rows 4 more times.

Row 53: As row 43, do not turn at the end of this row.

Body

The following is worked in rounds:

Rounds 1–4: Work 1 sc in each sc.

Round 5 (dec): (Sc2tog, 4 sc) 12 times (60 sts).

Rounds 6–8: Work 1 sc in each sc.

Round 9 (dec): (Sc2tog, 3 sc) 12 times (48 sts).

Rounds 10–12: Work 1 sc in each sc.

Round 13 (dec): (Sc2tog, 2 sc) 12 times (36 sts).

Rounds 14–16: Work 1 sc in each sc.

Round 17 (dec): (Sc2tog, 1 sc) 12 times (24 sts).

Rounds 18–20: Work 1 sc in each sc.

Round 21 (dec): (Sc2tog) 12 times (12 sts).

Rounds 22–24: Work 1 sc in each sc. Sl st to next st and fasten off, leaving a long length of yarn.

Shape neck
Rows 40–46

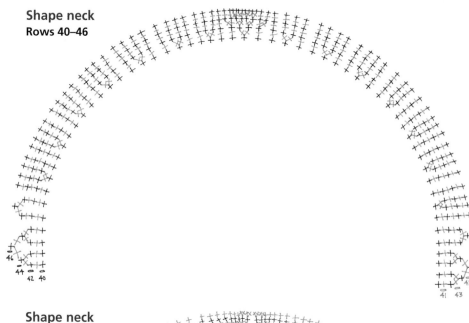

Shape neck
Rows 46–53

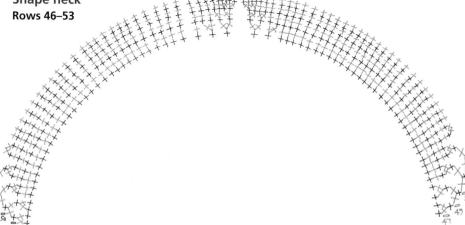

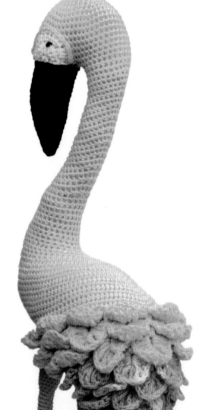

Beak

Starting at the tip of the beak, with C/2–D/3 hook and B, wind yarn around a finger a couple of times to form a ring, insert the hook, catch the yarn and draw back through the ring.

Round 1: Make 1 ch (does not count as a st), work 6 sc into ring (6 sts).

Round 2: Work 1 sc in each sc.

Round 3 (inc): (2 sc in next sc, 1 sc) 3 times, pull on short end of yarn to close ring (9 sts).

Round 4: Work 1 sc in each sc.

Round 5 (inc): (2 sc in next sc, 2 sc) 3 times (12 sts).

Round 6: Work 1 sc in each sc.

Round 7 (inc): (2 sc in next sc, 2 sc) 4 times (16 sts).

Round 8: Work 1 sc in each sc.

Round 9 (inc): (2 sc in next sc, 3 sc) 4 times (20 sts).

Shape beak

Round 10: 2 sc in next sc, 7 sc, (sc2tog) twice, 7 sc, 2 sc in next sc.

Rounds 11–12: Work 1 sc in each sc.

Round 13: As round 10.

Round 14 (inc): (2 sc in next sc, 4 sc) 4 times (24 sts).

Rounds 15–16: Work 1 sc in each sc.

Round 17: 2 sc in next sc, 9 sc, (sc2tog) twice, 9 sc, 2 sc in next sc.

Round 18: Work 1 sc in each sc.

Round 19: As round 17.

Round 20: As round 18.

Sl st to next st and fasten off.

Join beak to head

With right side facing and C/2–D/3 hook, join B to round 16 of the head where the work was divided for the beak, at the inside edge next to the neck. Insert the hook under both loops of the first sc of the head and then under both loops of the first sc of the beak, making sure the beak is placed so it curves under, toward the neck, rather than out. Work a single crochet to join the two stitches. Continue in this way, working together each sc from both pieces at the same time, being sure to insert the hook into a stitch of the head first and then the beak, so the stitches will form a decorative ridge that will lie toward the top of the head. Alternatively, the beak can be sewn in place.

flamingo

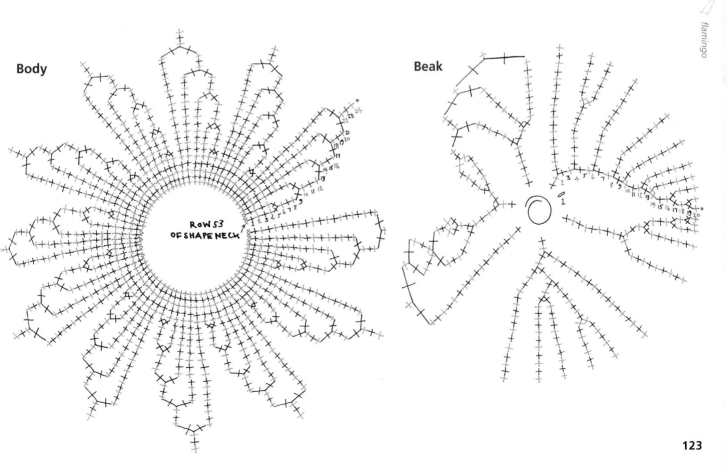

Body

ROW 53 OF SHAPE NECK

Beak

Eyes

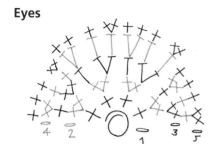

Eyes (make 2)

With C/2–D/3 hook and C, wind yarn around a finger a couple of times to form a ring, insert the hook, catch the yarn and draw back through the ring.

Row 1 (RS): 1 ch (does not count as a st), work 4 sc into ring, turn (4 sts).

Row 2 (inc): 1 ch (does not count as a st), (2 sc in next sc) 4 times, turn (8 sts).

Row 3 (inc): 1 ch (does not count as a st), 2 sc in next sc, 1 sc, (2 hdc in next st, 1 hdc) twice, 2 sc in next sc, 1 sc, turn (12 sts). Pull on short end of yarn to close ring.

Row 4 (inc): 1 ch (does not count as a st), 2 sc in same st, 2 sc, (2 hdc in next st, 2 hdc) twice, 2 sc in same st, 2 sc, turn (16 sts). Join yarn A.

Row 5 (inc): 1 ch, (does not count as a st), (2 sc in same st, 3 sc) 4 times, fasten off, leaving a long length of both yarns.

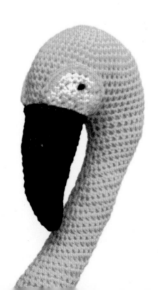

Upper leg

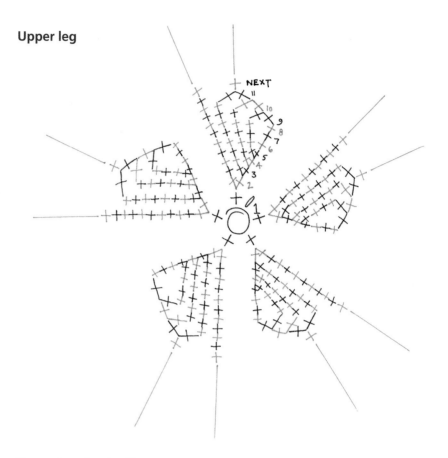

Upper legs (make 2)

Starting at the knee, with B/1–C/2 hook and E, winsd yarn around finger a couple of times to form a ring, insert the hook into the ring, catch the yarn and draw it back through the ring.

Round 1: 1 ch (does not count as a st, work 5 sc into ring (5 sts).

Round 2 (inc): (2 sc in next sc) 5 times (10 sts). Pull on short end of yarn to close ring.

Round 3 (inc): (2 sc in next sc, 1 sc) 5 times (15 sts).

Round 4 (inc): (2 sc in next sc, 2 sc) 5 times (20 sts).

Round 5 (inc): (2 sc in next sc, 3 sc) 5 times (25 sts).

Rounds 6–8: Work 1 sc in each sc.

Round 9 (dec): (Sc2tog, 3 sc) 5 times (20 sts).

Round 10 (dec): (Sc2tog, 2 sc) 5 times (15 sts).

Round 11 (dec): (Sc2tog, 1 sc) 5 times (10 sts).

Next: Work 1 sc in each st until upper leg measures 6½in (16.5cm) excluding knee.

Shape top of leg

Lower legs

Shape top of leg

Round 1 (inc): (2 sc in next sc, 1 sc) 5 times (15 sts).

Rounds 2–5: Work 1 sc in each sc.

Round 6 (inc): (2 sc in next sc, 2 sc) 5 times (20 sts).

Rounds 7–10: Work 1 sc in each sc.

Round 11 (inc): (2 sc in next sc, 3 sc) 5 times (25 sts).

Round 12: Work 1 sc in each sc. Sl st to next st and fasten off, leaving a long length of yarn at the end.

Lower legs (make 2)

Starting at the ankle, with B/1–C/2 hook and E, wind yarn around finger a couple of times to form a ring, insert the hook into the ring, catch the yarn and draw it back through the ring.

Round 1: 1 ch (does not count as a st), work 5 sc into ring (5 sts).

Round 2 (inc): (2 sc in next sc) 5 times (10 sts). Pull on short end of yarn to close ring.

Round 3: 1 sc in back loop only of each sc.

Next: Work 1 sc in both loops of each sc until the lower leg measures 8in (20cm) not including rounds 1 and 2. Sl st to next st and fasten off, leaving length of yarn.

Feet (make 2)

Starting at the heel, with B/1–C/2 hook and E, make 4 ch, join with a sl st to first ch to form a ring.

Round 1: 1 ch (does not count as a st), work 6 sc into ring (6 sts).

Round 2 (inc): (2 sc in next sc) 6 times (12 sts).

Round 3: Work 1 sc in each sc.

Round 4 (inc): (2 sc in next sc, 1 sc) 6 times (18 sts).

Round 5: Work 1 sc in each sc.

Round 6 (inc): (2 sc in next sc, 2 sc) 6 times (24 sts).

Round 7: Work 1 sc in each sc.

Round 8 (inc): (2 sc in next sc, 3 sc) 6 times (30 sts).

Round 9: Work 1 sc in each sc.

Round 10 (inc): (2 sc in next sc, 4 sc) 6 times (36 sts).

Round 11: Work 1 sc in each sc.

Round 12 (inc): (2 sc in next sc, 5 sc) 6 times (42 sts).

Round 13: Work 1 sc in each sc.

Round 14 (inc): (2 sc in next sc, 6 sc) 6 times (48 sts).

Round 15: Work 1 sc in each sc.

Round 16 (inc): (2 sc in next sc, 7 sc) 6 times (54 sts).

Round 17: Work 1 sc in each sc.

Feet
Rounds 1–17

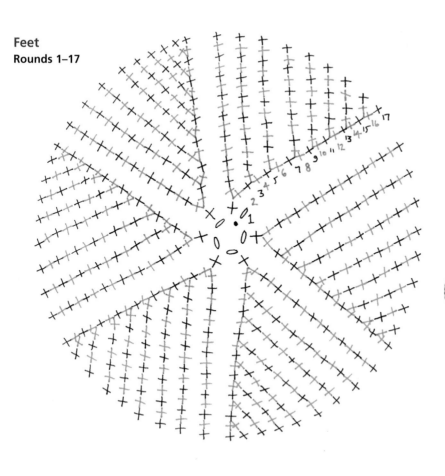

Shape toes

Round 1: Work 1 sc in each of next 9 sc, turn and work 1 sc in each of the 9 sc on the opposite side of the work. These 18 sts form the shaping of the first toe. Continue on these 18 sts:

Round 2 (dec): (Sc2tog, 1 sc) 6 times (12 sts).

Round 3 (dec): (Sc2tog, 2 sc) 3 times (9 sts).

Round 4: Work 1 sc in each sc.

Sl st to next st and fasten off, leaving a long length of yarn.

Rejoin yarn to the first sc of the remaining stitches on round 17 of the foot and rep rounds 1–4 to finish the next toe. Fasten off, leaving a length of yarn at the end. Work the final toe in the same way as before.

Shape toes

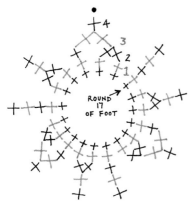

flamingo

DID YOU KNOW?

An adult flamingo's legs can be 30–50in (76–127cm) long, which is longer than their entire body.

Feathers
Rows 1–12

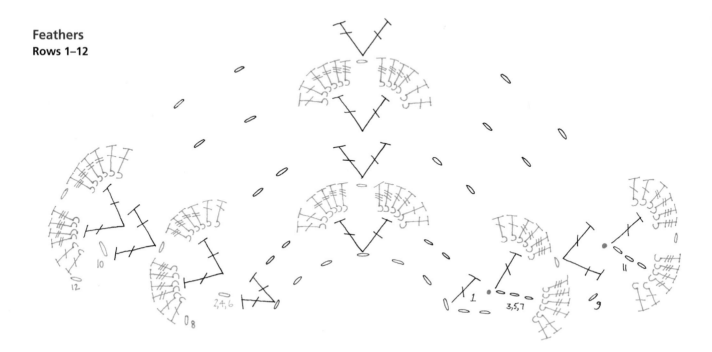

Feathers

With E/4 hook and D, make 9 ch.

Row 1: Work 1 dc into third ch from hook (counts as first 2 dc), (2 ch, sk 2 ch, 2 dc into next ch) twice (3 sets of 2 dc).

Row 2: 1 ch (does not count as a st), sk the first set of 2 dc, down the post of the first of the next 2 dc work 2 dc, 2 tr, 2 dtr, 1 ch, up the post of the second of 2 dc work 2 dtr, 2 tr, 2 dc, sk next set of 2 dc, sl st between last set of 2 dc (1 feather).

Row 3: 3 ch (counts as first dc), 1 dc between the 2 dc skipped on previous row, 2 ch, 2 dc into space in the center of the feather, 2 ch, 2 dc between the 2 dc skipped on previous row (3 sets of 2 dc).

Row 4: As row 2.

Rows 5–6: Rep rows 3 and 4.

Row 7: As row 3.

Row 8: 1 ch (does not count as a st), down the post of the first of 2 dc work 2 dc, 2 tr, 2 dtr, 1 ch, up the post of the second of 2 dc work 2 dtr, 2 tr, 2 dc, sk next set of 2 dc; down the post of the first of the next 2 dc work 2 dc, 2 tr, 2 dtr, 1 ch, up the post of the second of 2 dc work 2 dtr, 2 tr, 2 dc (2 feathers).

Row 9: 1 ch (does not count as a st), 2 dc into space in center of first feather, 2 ch, 2 dc in between the 2 dc skipped on previous row, 2 ch, 2 dc in center of next feather (3 sets of 2 dc).

Row 10: As row 2.

Row 11: As row 3.

Row 12: As row 8.

Feathers
Rows 11–17

flamingo

Row 13: 1 ch (does not count as a st), (2 dc, 2 ch, 2 dc) into space in center of first feather, 2 ch, 2 dc between the 2 dc skipped on previous row, 2 ch, (2 dc, 2 ch, 2 dc) into space in center of next feather (5 sets of 2 dc).

Row 14: 1 ch (does not count as a st), (down the post of the first of the next 2 dc work 2 dc, 2 tr, 2 dtr, 1 ch, up the post of the second of 2 dc work 2 dtr, 2 tr, 2 dc, sk next set of 2 dc) twice, down the post of the first of the next set of 2 dc work 2 dc, 2 tr, 2 dtr, 1 ch, up the post of the second of 2 dc work 2 dtr, 2 tr, 2 dc (3 feathers).

Row 15: 1 ch (does not count as a st), 2 dc into space in center of first feather, *2 ch, (2 dc, 2 ch, 2 dc) between the 2 dc skipped on previous row, 2 ch, 2 dc into space in center of next feather, repeat from * once (7 sets of 2 dc).

Row 16: 1 ch (does not count as a st), (down the post of the first of the next 2 dc work 2 dc, 2 tr, 2 dtr, 1 ch, up the post of the second of 2 dc work 2 dtr, 2 tr, 2 dc, sk next set of 2 dc) 3 times, down the post of the first of the next set of 2 dc work 2 dc, 2 tr, 2 dtr 1 ch, up the post of the second of 2 dc work 2 dtr, 2 tr, 2 dc (4 feathers).

129

Feathers
Rows 17–21

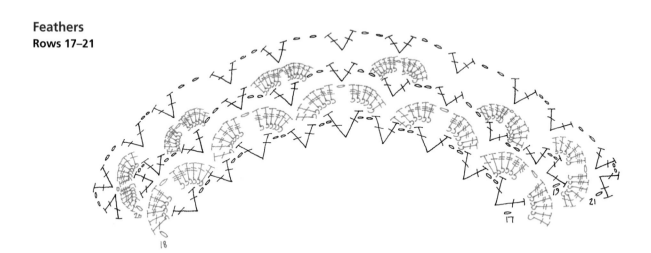

Row 17: 1 ch (does not count as a st), 2 dc into space in center of first feather, 2 ch, (2 dc, 2 ch, 2 dc) between the 2 dc skipped on previous row, 2 ch, 2 dc into space in center of next feather, 2 ch, 2 dc between the 2 dc skipped on previous row, 2 ch, 2 dc into space in center of next feather, 2 ch, (2 dc, 2 ch, 2 dc) between 2 dc skipped on previous row, 2 ch, 2 dc into space in center of next feather (9 sets of 2 dc).

Row 18: 1 ch (does not count as a st), (down the post of the first of the next 2 dc work 2 dc, 2 tr, 2 dtr, 1 ch, up the post of the second of 2 dc work 2 dtr, 2 tr, 2 dc sk next set of 2 dc) 4 times, down the post of the first of the next set of 2 dc work 2 dc, 2 tr, 2 dtr, 1 ch, up the post of the second of 2 dc work 2 dtr, 2 tr, 2 dc (5 feathers).

Row 19: 1 ch (does not count as a st), (2 dc, 2 ch, 2 dc) into space in center of first feather, 2 ch (2 dc between the 2 dc skipped on previous row, 2 ch, 2 dc into space in center of next feather, 2 ch) 4 times, 2 dc into space in center of the same feather (11 sets of 2 dc).

Row 20: 1 ch (does not count as a st), (down the post of the first of the next 2 dc work 2 dc, 2 tr, 2 dtr, 1 ch, up the post of the second of 2 dc work 2 dtr, 2 tr, 2 dc, sk next set of 2 dc) 5 times, down the post of the first of the next set of 2 dc work 2 dc, 2 tr, 2 dtr, 1 ch, up the post of the second of 2 dc work 2 dtr, 2 tr, 2 dc (6 feathers).

Row 21: 1 ch (does not count as a st), (2 dc, 2 ch, 2 dc) into space in center of first feather, 2 ch (2 dc between the 2 dc skipped on previous row, 2 ch, 2 dc into space in center of next feather, 2 ch) 5 times, 2 dc into space in center of same feather (13 sets of 2 dc).

Feathers
Rows 21–25

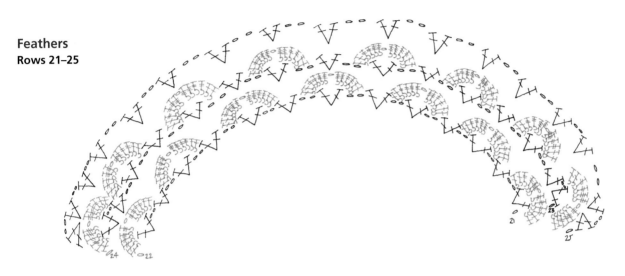

Row 22: 1 ch (does not count as a st), (down the post of the first of the next 2 dc work 2 dc, 2 tr, 2 dtr, 1 ch, up the post of the second of 2 dc work 2 dtr, 2 tr, 2 dc, sk next set of 2 dc) 6 times, down the post of the first of the next set of 2 dc work 2 dc, 2 tr, 2 dtr, 1 ch, up the post of the second of 2 dc work 2 dtr, 2 tr, 2 dc (7 feathers).

Row 23: 1 ch (does not count as a st), (2 dc, 2 ch, 2 dc) into space in center of first feather, 2 ch (2 dc between the 2 dc skipped on previous row, 2 ch, 2 dc into space in center of next feather, 2 ch) 6 times, 2 dc into space in center of same feather (15 sets of 2 dc).
Join and continue in yarn A.

Row 24: 1 ch (does not count as a st), (down the post of the first of the next 2 dc work 2 dc, 2 tr, 2 dtr, 1 ch, up the post of the second of 2 dc work 2 dtr, 2 tr, 2 dc, sk next set of 2 dc) 7 times, down the post of the first of the next set of 2 dc work 2 dc, 2 tr, 2 dtr, 1 ch, up the post of the second of 2 dc work 2 dtr, 2 tr, 2 dc (8 feathers).

DID YOU KNOW?
Flamingos rest by standing on one leg. The "knee" of the flamingo is actually an ankle joint and the lower leg bends forward from there.

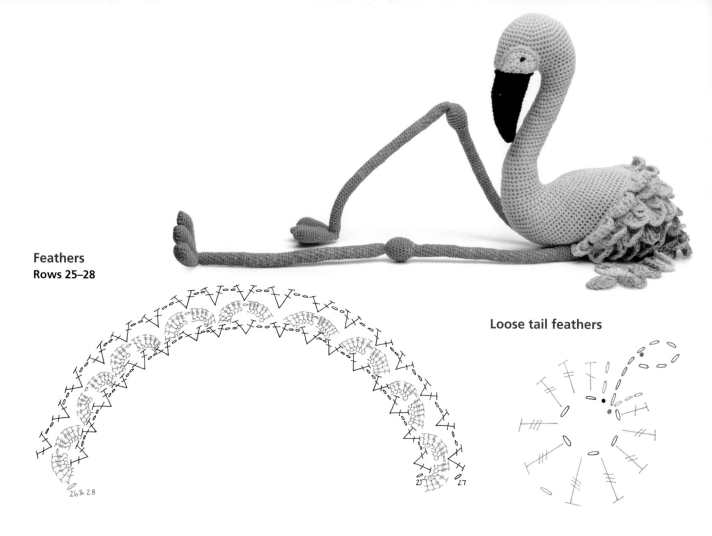

Feathers
Rows 25–28

Loose tail feathers

Row 25: 1 ch (does not count as a st), (2 dc, 2 ch, 2 dc) into space in center of first feather, 2 ch (2 dc between the 2 dc skipped on previous row, 2 ch, 2 dc into space in center of next feather, 2 ch) 7 times, 2 dc into space in center of same feather (17 sets of 2 dc).

Row 26: 1 ch (does not count as a st), (down the post of the first of the next 2 dc work 2 dc, 2 tr, 2 dtr, 1 ch, up the post of the second of 2 dc work 2 dtr, 2 tr, 2 dc sk next set of 2 dc) 8 times, down the post of the first of the next set of 2 dc work 2 dc, 2 tr, 2 dtr, 1 ch, up the post of the second of 2 dc work 2 dtr, 2 tr, 2 dc (9 feathers).

Row 27: 1 ch (does not count as a st), (2 dc into space in center of feather, 2 ch, 2 dc between the 2 dc skipped on previous row, 2 ch) 8 times, 2 dc into space in center of next feather (17 sets of 2 dc).
Row 28: As row 26.
Fasten off. Dampen with cold water and reshape the work, pulling the feathers so they lay flat. Lay out and leave to dry.

DID YOU KNOW?
A flock of flamingos is aptly called a flamboyance.

Loose tail feathers
With E/4 hook and D, make 6 ch and join with a sl st to first ch to form a ring.
Next: *2 ch (to count as first dc), into ring work 1 dc, 2 tr, 2 dtr, 1 ch, 2 dtr, 2 tr, 1 dc, 3 ch, sl st into ring, make 10 ch, sl st into sixth ch from hook to form a ring. Rep from * until 5 feathers have been completed, omitting the 10 ch at the end. To finish, make 5 ch and fasten off, leaving a long length of yarn. Dampen the work as before, reshape and leave to dry.

Finishing

Body

With the length of yarn left at the end of the body, run a gathering stitch around the opening, draw up to close and fasten off securely. Push the stuffing into the end of the body. Stuff the beak and head firmly, taking care to keep the curved shape of the beak. Neatly stitch the neck edges from the head end down to the body, matching the rows of stitches and leaving an opening of around 2in (5cm). Stuff the neck firmly, using a knitting needle or the end of a pencil to push the stuffing up the length to the top. Stitch another 1in (2.5cm) or so, leaving a small opening to push through the rest of the stuffing, firmly filling the chest and body of the bird, keeping a smooth and rounded shape. Close the seam and weave in the ends.

Eyes

Sew the eyes to each side of the face, butting the straight, lower edge of the eye against the edge of the beak and using the long lengths of white and pink yarn to stitch it neatly down. Work a French knot in B for the eyeball.

Feet

Stuff the feet lightly, pushing the stuffing through the openings at the toes. With the lengths of yarn left at the toes, run a gathering stitch around each opening, draw up to close and fasten off. Weave in the ends. With the same shade of yarn, work a simple running stitch through all the layers, starting from the heel and finishing in between each toe to form a quilted effect that defines the shaping.

Legs

Stuff the upper and lower legs firmly, using a long knitting needle or pencil to push the stuffing right to the ends and into the knee. Stitch the top end of the lower leg by squeezing it together and sewing the stitches from each side to form a straight seam. Do the same to join the stitches at the top of the upper leg. Sew the seam at the top of the lower leg to the knee so it faces the same way as the wide seam at the top of the upper leg. Position the top seam of the lower half of the leg so it sits centrally across the first couple of rounds of the knee. This will create a joint that will enable the leg to bend at the knee. Making sure the foot faces forward when the leg is bent at the knee joint, stitch the leg to the foot, sewing down all the stitches at the ankle. Sew the straight top end of the upper legs, positioning them next to each other around halfway down the underside of the body, with the feet facing toward the front of the flamingo.

Feathers

Use safety pins to temporarily attach the feathers in position over the flamingo, near the end of the body where the rows end and the rounds begin, after the neck shaping. You will see a difference in the texture of the fabric between the rows and rounds worked. Stitch in place across the last row of the feathers and work a few stitches further down the feathery tail and into the end of the body to hold it in place.

Thread the long length of yarn left after fastening off the loose tail feathers onto a needle and sew in place securely at the back of the work, between the two single end feathers, hanging from those stitched to the body. Weave in the yarn ends.

flamingo

Just like a real one, this chameleon really can change color! He doesn't have pigmented skin cells to do it for him though, so you need to turn him inside out through his mouth (see far right). Any shades of yarn can be combined to make this interesting lizard.

Chameleon

DID YOU KNOW?

Some chameleons change color as camouflage... Where's he gone?

Information you'll need

Finished size
Approximately 14½in (37cm) long

Materials
King Cole Mirage DK (or equivalent DK weight yarn, CYCA 3), 50% wool, 50% acrylic (343yds/312m per 100g ball)
1 x 100g ball in 876 Quebec (A)
1 x 100g ball in 865 Florence (B)
Scrap of DK yarn in black (C)
B/1–C/2 (UK12:2.5mm) and C/2–D/3 (UK11:3mm) crochet hooks
Toy stuffing
Darning needle
12 x 12in (30 x 30cm) batting

Gauge
22 sts and 24 rows to 4in (10cm) over single crochet using C/2–D/3 hook

Special stitch
Ridged stitch
With the right side of the work facing, insert the hook through to the back of the work, around the post of the previous ridged st and back through to the front, catch the yarn and draw the loop up to the level of the row being worked, catch the yarn again and draw through both loops on the hook to complete the ridged stitch.

chameleon

Key

 Wind yarn around finger to form a ring

✐ Chain (ch)

• Slip stitch (sl st)

+ Single crochet (sc)

ᐁᐧ 2 sc in same st

ᐧᐧ sc2tog

ᐧᐧᐧ 3 sc in same st

꒕ Ridged stitch

How to make Chameleon

Each piece is made in two colorways. The eyes and legs are crocheted in rounds, while the head and body are worked in rows of single crochet. The ridges going over the head and down the back are produced by working a single crochet into the post of the previous ridged stitch. The front and back pieces of each color are joined together at the end with the tail, which is worked in rounds. The two colored body pieces are joined by crocheting into each stitch of both pieces at the same time. Batting is used to help smooth out the body as the legs and tail of one colorway fills the inside. The sides of the front and back of the body are crocheted together, leaving the mouth open so the chameleon can be turned inside out to change the color. Finally, the eyes and legs are stitched to the head and body.

Front
Lower jaw

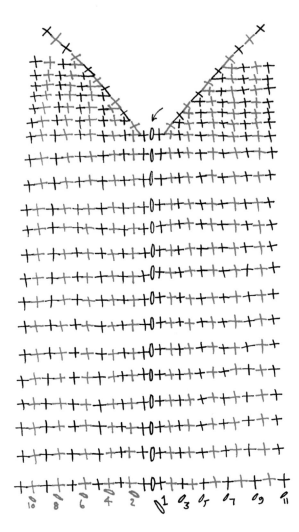

Front (make 1 in A and 1 in B)
Lower jaw
With C/2–D/3 hook, make 16 ch.
Row 1: 1 sc into second ch from hook, 1 sc into next 13 ch, 2 sc in end ch, 1 sc down reverse side of each chain to end, turn (30 sts).
Row 2 (inc): 1 ch (does not count as a st), 14 sc, (2 sc in next sc) twice, 14 sc, turn (32 sts).
Row 3 (inc): 1 ch (does not count as a st), 15 sc, (2 sc in next sc) twice, 15 sc, turn (34 sts).

Row 4 (inc): 1 ch (does not count as a st), 16 sc, (2 sc in next sc) twice, 16 sc, turn (36 sts).
Row 5 (inc): 1 ch (does not count as a st), 17 sc, (2 sc in next sc) twice, 17 sc, turn (38 sts).
Row 6 (inc): 1 ch (does not count as a st), 18 sc, (2 sc in next sc) twice, 18 sc, turn (40 sts).
Row 7 (inc): 1 ch (does not count as a st), 19 sc, (2 sc in next sc) twice, 19 sc, turn (42 sts).

Front Body

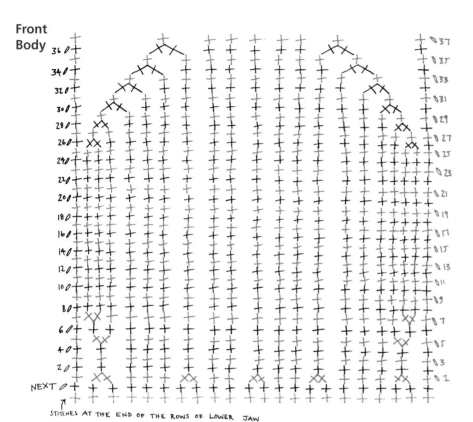

STITCHES AT THE END OF THE ROWS OF LOWER JAW

DID YOU KNOW?
Chameleons have a prehensile tail, which they can use to hold on to things. They also have a projectile tongue, the tip of which is a bulbous ball of muscle used to catch prey.

Row 8 (inc): 1 ch (does not count as a st), 20 sc, (2 sc in next sc) twice, 20 sc, turn (44 sts).

Rows 9–11: Work 1 sc in each sc, turn. Do not turn at the end of row 11.

Body

Next: 1 ch (does not count as a st), work 1 sc into each of the sts at the end of the 11 rows to the center of the lower jaw and then across the remaining 11 sts (22 sts).

Shape neck

Row 1 (RS) (dec): 1 ch (does not count as st), 1 sc, sc2tog, 3 sc, sc2tog, (2 sc, sc2tog) twice, 3 sc, sc2tog, 1 sc, turn (17 sts).

Rows 2–4: 1 ch (does not count as a st), work 1 sc in each sc, turn.

Shape front

Row 5 (inc): 1 ch (does not count as a st), 1 sc, 2 sc in next sc, 13 sc, 2 sc in next sc, 1 sc, turn (19 sts).

Row 6: 1 ch (does not count as a st), work 1 sc in each sc, turn.

Row 7 (inc): 1 ch (does not count as a st), 1 sc, 2 sc in next sc, 15 sc, 2 sc in next sc, 1 sc, turn (21 sts).

Rows 8–25: 1 ch (does not count as a st), work 1 sc in each sc, turn.

Row 26 (dec): 1 ch (does not count as a st), 1 sc, sc2tog, 15 sc, sc2tog, 1 sc, turn (19 sts).

Row 27: 1 ch (does not count as a st), work 1 sc in each sc, turn.

Row 28 (dec): 1 ch (does not count as a st), 1 sc, sc2tog, 13 sc, sc2tog, 1 sc, turn (17 sts).

Row 29: 1 ch (does not count as a st), work 1 sc in each sc, turn.

Row 30 (dec): 1 ch (does not count as a st), 1 sc, sc2tog, 11 sc, sc2tog, 1 sc, turn (15 sts).

Row 31: 1 ch (does not count as a st), work 1 sc in each sc, turn.

Row 32 (dec): 1 ch (does not count as a st), 1 sc, sc2tog, 9 sc, sc2tog, 1 sc, turn (13 sts).

Row 33: 1 ch (does not count as a st), work 1 sc in each sc, turn.

Row 34 (dec): 1 ch (does not count as a st), 1 sc, sc2tog, 7 sc, sc2tog, 1 sc, turn (11 sts).

Row 35: 1 ch (does not count as a st), work 1 sc in each sc, turn.

Row 36 (dec): 1 ch (does not count as st), 1 sc, sc2tog, 5 sc, sc2tog, 1 sc, turn (9 sts).

Row 37: 1 ch (does not count as a st), work 1 sc in each sc, turn.
Fasten off.

Back (make 1 in A and 1 in B)

Starting at center of top lip, with C/2–D/3 hook, wind yarn around a finger to form a ring, insert the hook, catch the yarn and draw back through the ring.

Row 1 (WS): 1 ch (does not count as a st), work 5 sc into ring, turn (5 sts).

Row 2 (RS) (inc): 1 ch (does not count as a st), (2 sc in next sc) twice, 1 sc, (2 sc in next sc) twice, turn. Pull on short end of yarn to close ring (9 sts).

Row 3 (inc): 1 ch (does not count as a st), (1 sc, 2 sc in next sc) 4 times, 1 sc, turn (13 sts).

Rows 4–5: 1 ch (does not count as a st), work 1 sc in each sc, turn.

Row 6: 1 ch (does not count as st), 1 sc in next 5 sc, work 1 ridged st around post of t next sc 2 rows down and bring loop up to level of working row, 1 sc, work 1 ridged st around post of next sc 2 rows down and bring loop up to level of working row, 1 sc into next 5 sc, turn.

Row 7 (inc): 1 ch (does not count as a st), 1 sc, 2 sc in next sc, 4 sc, 3 sc in next sc, 4 sc, 2 sc in next sc, 1 sc, turn (17 sts).

Row 8: 1 ch (does not count as a st), 6 sc, 1 ridged st, 3 sc, 1 ridged st, 6 sc, turn.

Row 9: 1 ch (does not count as a st), work 1 sc in each sc, turn.

Row 10: As row 8.

Row 11: 1 ch (does not count as a st), work 1 sc in each sc, turn.

Shape casque

Row 12: 1 ch (does not count as a st), 1 sc in next 6 sc, 1 ridged st, 1 sc, work 1 ridged st around post of the next sc two rows down, 1 sc, 1 ridged st, 6 sc, turn.

Back
Rows 1–24

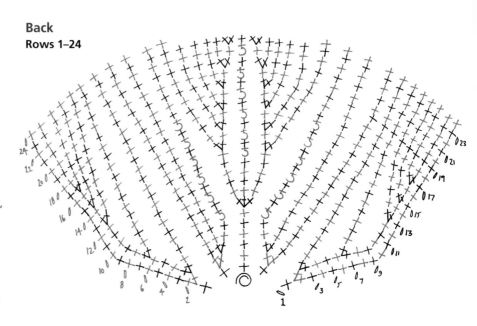

Row 13 (inc): 1 ch (does not count as a st), 1 sc, 2 sc in next sc, 5 sc, 2 sc in next sc, 1 sc, 2 sc in next sc, 5 sc, 2 sc in next sc, 1 sc, turn (21 sts).

Row 14: 1 ch (does not count as a st), 1 sc in next 7 sc, (1 ridged st, 2 sc) 3 times, 5 sc, turn.

Row 15 (inc): 1 ch (does not count as a st), 1 sc, 2 sc in next sc, 7 sc, 2 sc in next sc, 1 sc, 2 sc in next sc, 7 sc, 2 sc in next sc, 1 sc, turn (25 sts).

Row 16: 1 ch (does not count as a st), 1 sc in next 8 sc, 1 ridged st, (3 sc, 1 ridged st) twice, 8 sc, turn.

Row 17 (inc): 1 ch (does not count as a st), 1 sc, 2 sc in next sc, 9 sc, 2 sc in next sc, 1 sc, 2 sc in next sc, 9 sc, 2 sc in next sc, 1 sc, turn (29 sts).

Row 18: 1 ch (does not count as a st), 14 sc, 1 ridged st, 14 sc, turn.

Row 19 (inc): 1 ch (does not count as st), 13 sc, 2 sc in next sc, 1 sc, 2 sc in next sc, 13 sc, turn (31 sts).

Row 20: 1 ch (does not count as a st), 15 sc, 1 ridged st, 15 sc, turn.

Row 21 (inc): 1 ch (does not count as a st), 14 sc, 2 sc in next sc, 1 sc, 2 sc in next sc, 14 sc, turn (33 sts).

Row 22: 1 ch (does not count as a st), 16 sc, 1 ridged st, 16 sc, turn.

Row 23 (inc): 1 ch (does not count as a st), 15 sc, 2 sc in next sc, 1 sc, 2 sc in next sc, 15 sc, turn (35 sts).

Row 24: 1 ch (does not count as a st), 11 sc, sk the next 13 sc, 11 sc, turn (22 sts).

Shape neck

Row 25 (dec): 1 ch (does not count as a st), 1 sc, sc2tog, 3 sc, sc2tog, (2 sc, sc2tog) twice, 3 sc, sc2tog, 1 sc, turn (17 sts).

Rows 26–27: 1 ch (does not count as a st), work 1 sc in each sc, turn.

Row 28: 1 ch (does not count as a st), 8 sc, work 1 ridged st around the post of the next sc 2 rows down and bring the loop up to the level of the working row, 8 sc, turn.

Shape back

Row 29 (inc): 1 ch (does not count as a st), 1 sc, 2 sc in next sc, (2 sc, 2 sc in next sc) twice, 1 sc, (2 sc in next sc, 2 sc) twice, 2 sc in next sc, 1 sc, turn (23 sts).

Row 30: 1 ch (does not count as a st), 11 sc, 1 ridged st, 11 sc, turn.

Row 31 (inc): 1 ch (does not count as a st), 1 sc, (2 sc in next sc, 3 sc) 5 times, 2 sc in next sc, 1 sc, turn (29 sts).

Row 32: 1 ch (does not count as a st), 14 sc, 1 ridged st, 14 sc, turn.

Row 33 (inc): 1 ch (does not count as a st), 1 sc, 2 sc in next sc, (4 sc, 2 sc in next sc) twice, 5 sc, (2 sc in next sc, 4 sc) twice, 2 sc in next sc, 1 sc, turn (35 sts).

Row 34: 1 ch (does not count as a st), 17 sc, 1 ridged st, 17 sc, turn.

Row 35: 1 ch (does not count as a st), work 1 sc in each sc, turn.

Rows 36–45: Repeat last 2 rows 5 more times.

Row 46: As row 34.

Row 47 (dec): 1 ch (does not count as a st), 1 sc, sc2tog, (4 sc, sc2tog) twice, 5 sc, (sc2tog, 4 sc) twice, sc2tog, 1 sc, turn (29 sts).

Row 48: As row 32.

Row 49: 1 ch (does not count as a st), work 1 sc in each sc, turn.

Back
Rows 24–61

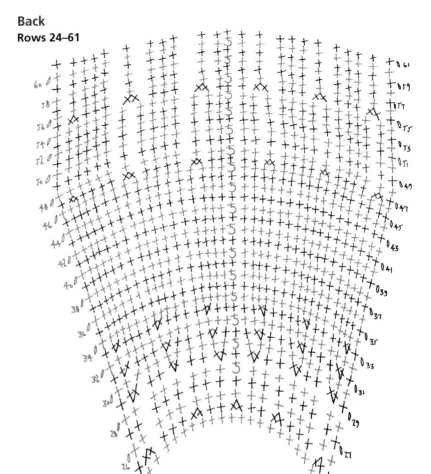

Rows 50–53: Repeat the last 2 rows twice.

Row 54: As row 32.

Row 55 (dec): 1 ch (does not count as a st), 1 sc, (sc2tog, 3 sc) 5 times, sc2tog, 1 sc, turn (23 sts).

Row 56: As row 30.

Row 57: 1 ch (does not count as a st), work 1 sc in each sc, turn.

Rows 58–61: Repeat the last 2 rows twice.

chameleon

Tail
Rows 61 of back and 37 of front
Rounds 62–77

Tail
Rounds 77–89

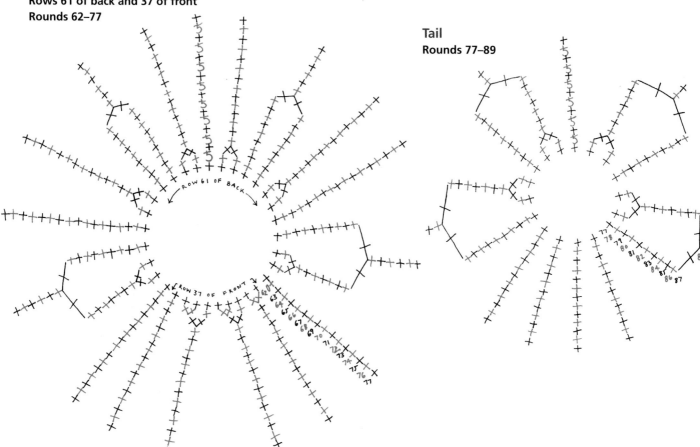

Tail

The following is worked in rounds:

Round 62: 1 ch (does not count as a st), 11 sc, 1 ridged st, 11 sc, working into the last row of the front piece with right side facing, 1 sc in the first sc to join one side, (sc2tog, 1 sc) twice, sc2tog (29 sts)

Round 63 (dec): 1 sc into the first sc of the back to join the other side, sc2tog, (2 sc, sc2tog) twice, 1 sc, (sc2tog, 2 sc) 3 times, (sc2tog) twice, 1 sc (21 sts).

Round 64: Work 1 sc in next 8 sc, 1 ridged st, work 1 sc in next 12 sc.

Round 65: Work 1 sc in each sc.

Rounds 66–69: Repeat last 2 rounds twice.

Round 70: As round 64.

Round 71 (dec): 1 sc, (sc2tog, 2 sc) twice, 1 sc, (sc2tog, 2 sc) twice, 3 sc (17 sts).

Round 72: Work 1 sc in next 6 sc, 1 ridged st, 1 sc in next 10 sc.

Round 73: Work 1 sc in each sc.

Rounds 74–77: Repeat last 2 rounds twice.

Round 78: As round 72.

Round 79 (dec): (1 sc, sc2tog) 4 times, 5 sc (13 sts).

Round 80: Work 1 sc in next 4 sc, 1 ridged st, 1 sc in next 8 sc.

Round 81: Work 1 sc in each sc.

Rounds 82–85: Repeat last 2 rounds twice.

Round 86: As round 80.

Round 87 (dec): (Sc2tog) twice, 1 sc, (sc2tog) twice, 4 sc (9 sts).

Round 88: Work 1 sc in next 2 sc, 1 ridged st, 1 sc in next 6 sc.

Round 89: Work 1 sc in each sc.

Rounds 90–95: Repeat last 2 rounds 3 more times.

Rounds 96–130: Work 1 sc in each sc. Fasten off, leaving a long length of yarn.

Tail
Rounds 89–130

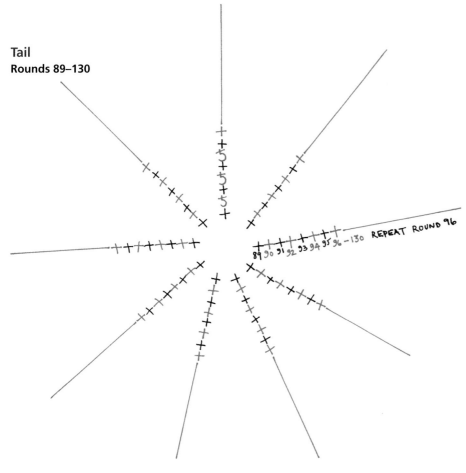

REPEAT ROUND 96
89 90 91 92 93 94 95 96 – 130

Eyeballs

Eye sockets

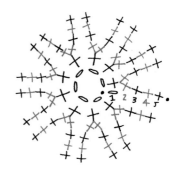

Eyeballs (make 4)
With B/1–C/2 hook and C, wind yarn around a finger a couple of times to form a ring, insert the hook, catch the yarn and draw back through the ring.
Round 1: 1 ch (does not count as a st), work 6 sc into ring (6 sts).
Round 2 (inc): (2 sc in next sc) 6 times.

Pull on short end of yarn to close ring (12 sts).
Round 3 (inc): (2 sc in next sc, 1 sc) 6 times (18 sts).
Round 4: Work 1 sc in each sc. Sl st to next st and fasten off.

Eye sockets (make 2 in A and 2 in B)
With C/2–D/3 hook, make 6 ch and join with a sl st to first ch to form a ring.
Round 1: 1 ch (does not count as a st), work 9 sc into ring (9 sts).
Round 2 (inc): (2 sc in next sc) 9 times (18 sts).
Rounds 3–5: Work 1 sc in each sc. Sl st to next st and fasten off, leaving a long length of yarn.

Front and back legs
Rounds 1–5

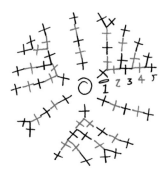

Legs
Divide legs

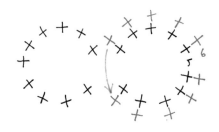

Front legs
(make 2 in A and 2 in B)

Starting at elbow, with B/1–C/2 hook, wind yarn around a finger to form ring, insert the hook, catch the yarn and draw back through the ring.

Round 1: 1 ch (does not count as a st), work 6 sc into ring (6 sts).

Round 2 (inc): (2 sc in next sc, 1 sc) 3 times. Pull on short end of yarn to close ring (9 sts).

Round 3 (inc): (2 sc in next sc, 2 sc) 3 times (12 sts).

Round 4 (inc): (2 sc in next sc, 3 sc) 3 times (15 sts).

Round 5 (inc): (2 sc in next sc, 2 sc) 5 times (20 sts).

Divide for upper and lower leg

Round 6: Work 1 sc into next 5 sc, turn and work 1 sc into the opposite 5 sc. Continue on these 10 sts for the lower part of the leg.

Rounds 7–25: Work 1 sc in each of the 10 sc.

Round 26 (inc): (2 sc in next sc, 4 sc) twice (12 sts).

Round 27 (inc): (2 sc in next sc, 2 sc) 4 times (16 sts).

Legs
Rounds 6–25

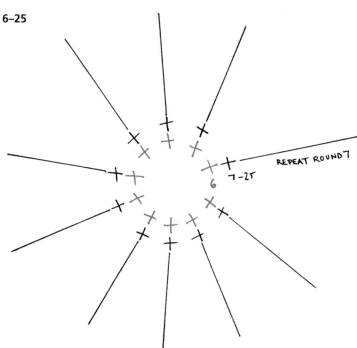

Legs
Rounds 25–27

Divide for foot

Round 28: Work 1 sc into next 4 sc, turn and work 1 sc into the opposite 4 sc (8 sts).

Foot

Work 4 rounds of 1 sc in each of the 8 sc. Fasten off, leaving a length of yarn. Rejoin yarn to the remaining 8 sts at the foot and work 5 rounds of 1 sc in each sc. Fasten off, leaving a length of yarn. Stuff the lower leg and foot, using the end of the crochet hook to push the stuffing down, keeping them soft so they are flexible enough to be tucked back easily into the chameleon when it is turned inside out to change color.

Upper leg

Rejoin yarn to the remaining 10 sts of round 5 at the elbow and work 11 rounds of 1 sc in each sc. Fasten off, leaving a length of yarn at the end. Stuff the upper leg.

Legs
Divide for foot

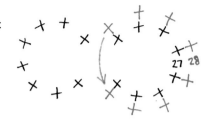

Foot

Upper leg
Work 11 rounds for front legs and 14 rounds for back legs

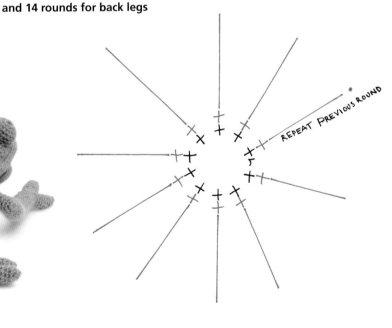

Joining the two colors

Back legs (make 2 in A and 2 in B)
Starting at the elbow, with B/1–C/2 hook, wind yarn around a finger a couple of times to form a ring, insert the hook, catch the yarn and draw back through the ring.

Next: Work rounds 1–28 as for front legs.

Foot
Work as for front legs.

Upper leg
Rejoin yarn to the remaining 10 sts of round 5 at the elbow and work 14 rounds of 1 sc in each sc. Sl st to next st and fasten off leaving a long length of yarn at the end. Stuff the upper leg.

ALL CHANGE!
Some chameleons can change in color in 20 seconds. Ours takes a little longer, as you have to turn him inside out.

Finishing

Stuff the tail, pushing it in through the narrow end with the crochet hook and filling it from the wider end as well. Keep it soft enough to roll up easily. Thread the length of yarn left after fastening off the tail onto a blunt-ended darning needle and thread through the last round of stitches, draw up to gather and stitch to secure. Curl the tail under at the end, stitching it down as you roll it for around the first 10in (25cm). Repeat for the other colored piece.

Join the two colored body pieces

Cut the batting to the shapes of the front and the back pieces excluding the tail and the casque. They don't have to be exact and a perfect fit. Lay out the back and front in A with wrong side facing up. Place the batting on the top and then lay the wrong side of the piece in B over the batting. Pin in place, matching the rows (see photograph at top of opposite page). Using C/2–D/3 hook and A, rejoin the yarn to the center of the top lip. With the body in yarn A facing you, work 1 sc into the stitches at the end of each row of both pieces at the same time to join. Insert the hook first into the body worked in A and then into the body worked in B and work down the 61 stitches of one side of the back to the tail, 37 sts down the front, work 1 sc into each of the 44 stitches of the lower jaw and then up the 37 stitches of the other side of the front and the 61 stitches of the other side of the back. Sl st into the first sc and fasten off. Weave in the ends. (240 sts.)

Cut triangular-shaped pieces of batting to fit inside each casque. Put a couple of folded pieces of batting together for each to help them stand and sew each side of the opening together in matching yarn to close.

Join front to back

Fold the body over, with yarn A facing out and B on the inside. Rejoin yarn A to the tail end and, with front facing, work 1 sc into each of the next 39 sc of both the front and back at the same time to join, inserting the hook under both loops of each stitch and finishing at the mouth. Continue working 1 sc into each of the next 44 sc of the top lip only and then join the other side of the body, working 1 sc into each of the next 39 sc of both the front and back at the same time to join as before. Fasten off. Rejoin yarn A to the remaining stitches on the lower lip and, with the inside of the mouth facing you, work 1 sc into each of the next 40 stitches. Change to B/1–C/2 hook and work 1 sc into each of the 44 sc around the top lip and then into the 40 sc around the lower lip. Sl st to the first sc, fasten off and weave in the ends.

Eyes

Push the eyeballs into each eye socket. With the length of yarn left after fastening off the eye socket, stitch the lower edges together. Stuff the eyes and sew in place to the head, stitching all around the lower edges to attach them securely.

Legs

With the lengths of yarn left after fastening off at the feet, run a gathering stitch through the last rounds at the openings, draw up to close and work a few stitches through to secure. Sew the legs in place, just above the line of single crochet that joins the front and back of the body, stitching all around the open end.

Changing color

To change the color of the chameleon, reach into the mouth and grasp hold of the tail inside. Carefully fold back the head, bringing the tail to the outside. Tuck in the legs that are going back into the body as it is turned right side out. Fold the mouth down and pull into shape.

How do snakes keep so slim?

Why do monkeys keep hanging around?

Do giraffes get vertigo?

Where do polar bears go for swimming lessons?

Techniques

Getting started

When starting a project, read the list of materials required at the beginning of the pattern. This will give you the size of hook and amount of yarn, as well as other items that are needed to make each animal.

Gauge

Checking the gauge before starting a project is vital, as this will affect the size and look of the finished piece. The gauge is the number of rounds or rows and stitches per square inch or centimeter of crocheted fabric.

Using the same size hook and stitch that the gauge has been measured over in the pattern, work a sample of around 5in (12.5cm) and then smooth it out on a flat surface. Place a ruler horizontally across the work and mark 4in (10cm) with pins. Count the number of stitches between the pins, including half stitches. This will give you the gauge of stitches.

Measure the gauge of rounds/rows by placing a ruler vertically over the work and mark 4in (10cm) with pins. Count the number of rounds/rows between the pins. If the number of stitches and rounds/rows is greater than those stated in the pattern, your gauge is tighter and you should use a larger hook. If the number of stitches and rounds/rows is less than those stated in the pattern, your gauge is looser, so you should use a smaller hook.

Hooks

Sizes vary widely, from tiny hooks that produce a very fine stitch when used with threads, to oversized hooks for working with several strands of yarn at one time to create a bulky fabric. Using a larger or smaller hook will change the look of the fabric and will also affect the gauge and the amount of yarn required.

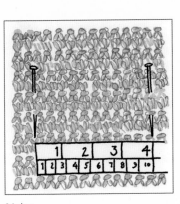

Stitches

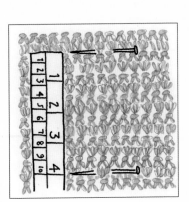

Rounds/rows

techniques

Needles

Blunt-ended darning or tapestry needles are used to sew the projects together. The rounded end will prevent any snagging and the large eye makes it easy to thread the needle with the thicker yarns. Embroidery needles come in several sizes and types. Two of them used in this book are the embroidery needle, which has a slightly elongated eye and a sharp point to go through the fabric; and the tapestry needle, which has a long eye and blunt end used for projects that do not pierce the fabric. Sewing needles also come in a variety of sizes and are used here for stitching buttons and beads to finish the features of some of the wild animals.

Substituting yarns

When substituting yarns, it is important to calculate the number of balls required by the number of yards or meters per ball rather than the weight of the yarn, as this varies according to the fiber. Gauge is also important. Work a gauge swatch in the yarn you wish to use before starting a project. Here is a list of the yarns used in the projects and the information that will help when substituting the yarn, including the gauge and a guide to the approximate hook size recommended by the manufacturers. **Note:** the manufacturers' suggestions on gauge and hook size listed here sometimes vary from those stated in the patterns. This may be, for example, to achieve a looser or denser crocheted fabric than is usually created with that yarn.

Camel and Giraffe

Rico Design Essentials Merino DK (or equivalent DK weight yarn, CYCA 3), 100% merino wool (131yds/120m per 50g ball)
Gauge: 22 sts and 28 rows to 4in (10cm)
Hook size: USG/6–7 (UK8–7:4–4.5mm)

Chameleon

King Cole Mirage DK (or equivalent DK weight yarn, CYCA 3), 50% wool, 50% acrylic (343yds/312m per 100g ball)
Gauge: 22 sts and 28 rows to 4in (10cm)
Hook size: USG/6 (UK8:4mm)

Deer

Rowan Handknit Cotton (or equivalent Worsted weight yarn, CYCA 4), 100% cotton (93yds/85m per 50g ball)
Gauge: 19–20 sts and 28 rows to 4in (10cm)
Hook size: USG/6–7 (UK8–7:4–4.5mm)

Elephant

Sirdar Snuggly DK (or equivalent DK weight yarn, CYCA 3), 55% nylon, 45% acrylic (179yds/165m per 50g ball)
Gauge: 22 sts and 28 rows to 4in (10cm)
Hook size: USG/6 (UK8:4mm)

Flamingo

Sirdar Calico DK (or equivalent DK weight yarn, CYCA 3), 60% cotton, 40% acrylic (172yds/158m per 50g ball)
Gauge: 22 sts and 28 rows to 4in (10cm)
Hook size: USG/6 (UK8:4mm)
Sirdar Snuggly Smiley Stripes DK (or equivalent DK weight yarn, CYCA 3), 80% bamboo (sourced viscose), 20% wool (104yds/95m per 50g ball)
Gauge: 22 sts and 28 rows to 4in (10cm)
Hook size: USG/6 (UK8:4mm)
Patons 100% Cotton 4ply (or equivalent Sport weight yarn, CYCA 2), 100% cotton (361yds/330m per 100g ball)
Gauge: 28 sts and 36 rows to 4in (10cm)
Hook size: USD/3 (UK10:3.25mm)

Fox, Frog, and Monkey

Adriafil Regina, 100% merino wool (or equivalent DK weight yarn, CYCA 3) (137yds/125m per 50g ball)
Gauge: 20 sts and 29 rows to 4in (10cm)
Hook size: US7 (UK7:4.5mm)

Lion and Snake

King Cole Merino Blend DK (or equivalent DK weight yarn, CYCA 3), 100% wool (123yds/112m per 50g ball)
Gauge: 22 sts and 28 rows to 4in (10cm)
Hook size: USG/6 (UK8:4mm)

Owl

Bergère de France Baronval (or equivalent DK weight yarn, CYCA 3), 60% wool, 40% acrylic (137yds/125m per 50g ball)
Gauge: 22 sts and 29 rows to 4in (10cm)
Hook size: USC/2–E/4 (UK11–9:3–3.5mm)
Bergère de France Lavandou (or equivalent DK weight yarn, CYCA 3), 59% acrylic, 30% cotton, 11% polyester (142yds/130m per 50g ball)
Gauge: 22 sts and 30 rows to 4in (10cm)
Hook size: USE/4 (UK9:3.5mm)

Polar Bear and Rabbit

Bergère de France Lima (or equivalent Sport weight yarn, CYCA 2), 80% wool, 20% alpaca (120yds/110m per 50g ball)
Gauge: 24 sts and 30 rows to 4in (10cm)
Hook size: USC/2–E/4 (UK11–9:3–3.5mm)

Reading charts

Each symbol on a chart represents a stitch; each round or horizontal row represents one round or row of crochet. For rounds of crochet, read the chart counterclockwise, starting at the center and working out to the last round on the chart.

Crochet stitches

Crochet is produced with one working loop on the hook—unlike knitting, where there are several or many stitches on the needle. Basic crochet stitches form various interesting patterns and fabrics when combined with each other and worked with different types of yarn.

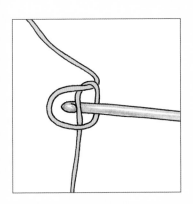

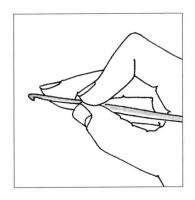

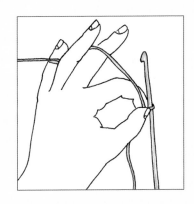

Slip knot

Take the end of the yarn and form it into a ring. Holding it in place between thumb and forefinger, insert the hook through the ring, catch the long end that is attached to the ball, and draw it back through. Keeping the yarn looped on the hook, pull through until the loop closes around the hook, ensuring it is not tight. Pulling on the short end of yarn will loosen the knot; pulling on the long end will tighten it.

Holding the hook

Hold the hook as you would a pencil, bringing your middle finger forward to rest near the tip of the hook. This will help control the movement of the hook, while the fingers of your other hand will regulate the tension of the yarn. The hook should face you, pointing slightly downward. The motion of the hook and yarn should be free and even, not tight. This will come with practice.

Holding the yarn

To hold your work and control the tension, pass the yarn over the first two fingers of your left hand (right if you are left-handed), under the third finger, around the little finger, and let the yarn fall loosely to the ball. As you work, take the stitch you made between the thumb and forefinger of the same hand.

The hook is usually inserted through the top 2 loops of a stitch as you work, unless otherwise stated in a pattern. A different effect is produced when only the back loop of the stitch is picked up.

Chain (ch)

1 Pass the hook under and over the yarn that is held taut between the first and second fingers. This is called "yarn over" (yo). Draw the yarn through the loop on the hook. This makes one chain.

2 Repeat step 1 until you have as many chain stitches as required, keeping the thumb and forefinger of the left hand close to the hook.

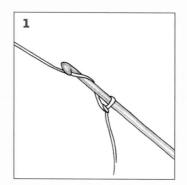

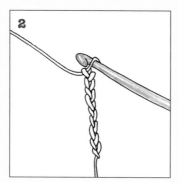

Slip stitch (sl st)

Make a practice chain of 10.

Insert hook into first stitch, yrh, draw through both loops on hook. This forms 1 slip stitch.

Continue to end. This will give you 10 slip stitches (10 sts).

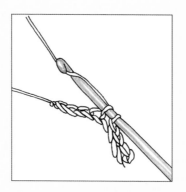

Single crochet (sc)

Make a practice chain of 17. Skip the first chain.

1 Insert hook from front into the next stitch, yarn over and draw back through the stitch (2 loops on hook).

2 Yarn over and draw through 2 loops (1 loop on hook). This makes one single crochet. Repeat steps 1 and 2 to end.

On the foundation chain of 17 stitches you should have 16 single crochet stitches (16 sts).

Next row
Turn the work so the reverse side faces you. Make 1 chain. This is the turning chain, which helps keep a neat edge and does not count as a stitch. Repeat steps 1 and 2 to the end of the row. Continue until the desired number of rows is complete. Fasten off.

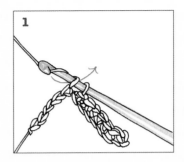

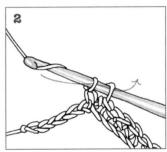

Half double (hdc)

Make a practice chain of 17. Skip the first 2 chain (these count as the first half double stitch).

1 Yarn over, insert hook into the next st, yarn over and draw back through stitch (3 loops on hook).

2 Yarn over, draw through all 3 loops (1 loop on hook). This forms 1 half double (hdc).

Repeat steps 1 and 2 to the end of the row.

On the foundation chain of 17 stitches you should have 16 half double stitches (16 sts), including the 2 chain at the beginning of the row, which is counted as the first stitch.

Next row
Turn the work so the reverse side faces you. Make 2 chain to count as the first half double. Skip the first stitch of the previous row. Repeat steps 1 and 2 for the next 14 hdc of the last row, work 1 hdc in the second of the 2 chain at the end of the row. Continue until the desired number of rows is complete. Fasten off.

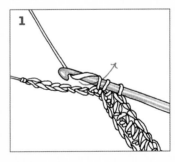

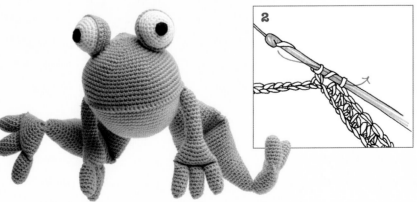

Double crochet (dc)

Make a practice chain of 18. Skip the first 3 chain (these count as the first double crochet stitch).

1 Yarn over, insert hook into the next stitch, yarn over and draw back through stitch (3 loops on hook).

2 Yarn over, draw through 2 loops (2 loops on hook).

3 Yarn over, draw through 2 loops (1 loop on hook). This forms 1 double crochet (dc). Repeat steps 1–3 to end of row.

On the foundation chain of 18 stitches you should have 16 double crochet stitches (16 sts), including the 3 chain at the beginning of the row, counted as the first stitch.

Next row
Turn the work so the reverse side faces you. Make 3 chain to count as the first double crochet. Skip the first stitch of the previous row. Repeat steps 1–3 to the end of the row, working 1 double crochet into the third of the 3 chain at the beginning of the last row. Continue until the desired number of rows is complete. Fasten off.

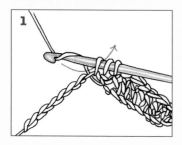
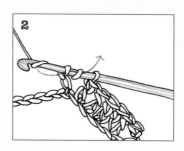
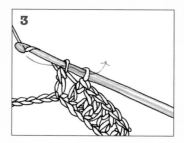

Treble (tr)

Make a practice chain of 19. Skip the first 4 chain (these count as the first treble stitch).

1 Yarn over twice, insert hook into the next stitch, yarn over and draw back through stitch (4 loops on hook).

2 (Yarn over, draw through 2 loops) three times (1 loop on hook). This forms 1 treble (tr).

Repeat steps 1 and 2 to end of row. On the foundation chain of 19 stitches you will have 16 trebles (16 sts), including the 4 chain at the start, counted as the first stitch.

Next row Turn the work so the reverse side faces you. Make 4 chain to count as the first tr. Skip the first stitch of the previous row. Repeat steps 1 and 2 to the end of the row. Continue until you have completed the desired number of rows. Fasten off.

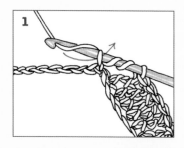
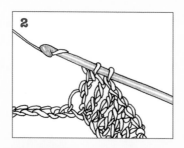

Double treble (dtr)

Make a practice chain of 20. Skip the first 5 chain (these count as the first double treble stitch).

1 Yarn over three times, insert hook into the next stitch, yarn over and draw back through stitch (5 loops on hook).

2 (Yarn over, draw through 2 loops) four times (1 loop on hook). This forms 1 double treble (dtr).

Repeat steps 1 and 2 to end of the row. On the foundation chain of 20 sts you should have 16 double trebles (16 sts), including the 5 chain at the beginning of the row, counted as the first stitch.

Next row
Turn the work so the reverse side faces you. Make 5 chain to count as the first dtr. Skip the first stitch of the previous row. Repeat steps 1 and 2 in each stitch to the end of the row. Continue until you have completed the desired number of rows. Fasten off.

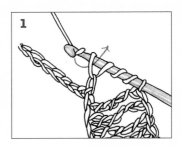

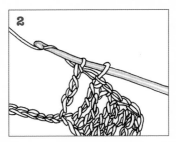

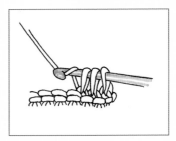

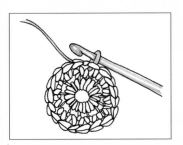

Joining in colors

When joining a new color in a continuous round, insert the hook into the first stitch of the next round, catch the yarn in the new color and draw through the stitch. Work the first stitch in the new color into the same place as the join.

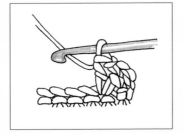

Increasing

To increase one single crochet (2 sc in next st), half double (2 hdc in next st) or double crochet stitch (2 dc in next st), work two stitches into one stitch of the previous row. To increase two single crochet stitches (3 sc in next st), simply work three stitches into one stitch of the previous row.

Decreasing

To decrease one single crochet (sc2tog), insert the hook into the next stitch, yarn over and draw back through the stitch (2 loops on hook); insert the hook into the following stitch, yarn over and draw back through the stitch (3 loops on hook), yarn over and draw through all three loops on the hook.

Fastening off

When you have finished, fasten off by cutting the yarn around 4¾in (12cm) from the work. Draw the loose end through the remaining loop, pulling it tightly.

Finishing touches

The animals begin to take shape when joining the seams and stuffing the crocheted pieces. However, it is the embroidery and stitching of the features that gives them an individual character that really brings them to life.

Seams

When stitching up your work, use clothespins or safety pins to hold the pieces together. Here are a couple of seams that can be used to finish off the crocheted projects.

Right side seam
This method produces a strong, flat, and invisible seam. It is used when joining pieces on the right side of the work, as for the neck of the Flamingo.

1 With wrong sides of the work together, attach the yarn to one piece of the work to be joined, insert the needle in from the back to the front of the other piece of the work, catching one loop of the edge stitch. Then insert the needle a little further along the same piece of the work, from the front to the back, and draw up the yarn tightly.

2 Insert the needle into the first piece of the work from the front to the back, catching one loop of the edge stitch as before. Then insert the needle a little further along the same edge from the back to the front of the work and draw up the yarn tightly. Continue in this way to the end.

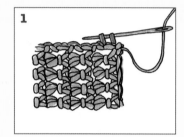

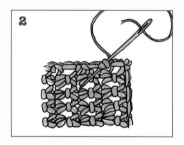

Woven flat seam
This brings the edges of the seam together, creating a neat and flat finish. With right sides together and matching the stitches at the edge of the work, place a finger

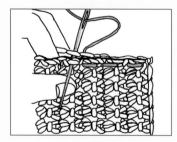

between the two pieces to be joined. Insert the needle from the front to the back, through both pieces under the loops of the corresponding stitches at the edge of the work. Then insert the needle from the back to the front of both pieces, pulling the yarn through to draw the seam together. Work in and out of each stitch to the end.

Stuffing

Polyester stuffing is a synthetic fiber that is lightweight and washable. Pure wool stuffing is a lovely, natural fiber. Durable and soft, it can be washed by hand but cannot be machine-washed as it will shrink and felt. Kapok is a natural fiber with a soft, silky texture. It comes from a seedpod that is harvested from the Ceiba tree.

Before stuffing your wild animals, tease the fibers by pulling them apart with your fingers to make them light and fluffy. This will prevent the crocheted piece from looking lumpy. Use small amounts at a time and build up the filling. The blunt end of a knitting needle, crochet hook, or a pencil is useful for pushing the stuffing into hard-to-reach areas such as tails and legs.

Embroidery stitches

Many of the animals are finished off with embroidered details to create features and impart character. Here are some commonly used embroidery stitches.

French knot

1 Bring the thread through to the right side of the work at the desired position the French knot is to be made and hold it down with the left thumb. Wind the thread twice around the needle, still holding it firmly in place.

2 Insert the needle back into the work, close to the point where the thread first appeared. Pull the thread through to tighten the knot and bring the needle back through to the front of the work to start another French knot.

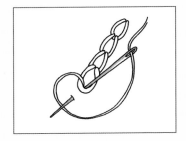

Chain stitch

Bring the thread through to the right side of the work at the position where the stitch is to be made and hold it down with your left thumb. Insert the needle where it first came out and bring it back through a little way from the last point, according to the length of the stitch you wish to make. Pull through, keeping the thread under the needle. Repeat to continue the chain.

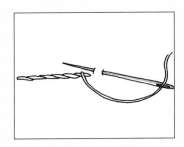

Stem stitch

Start by making a tiny stitch. Work from left to right, bringing the needle through the outline to the center of the stitch. Keep the stitches small and the thread below the needle. The stitches are slightly slanted and work well on curved lines.

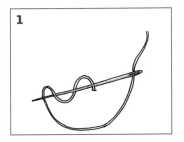

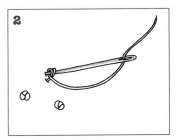

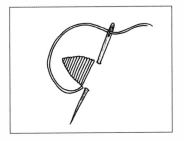

Satin stitch

Work straight stitches side by side and close together across a shape. Take care to keep the stitches even and the edge neat. The finished result will look like satin.

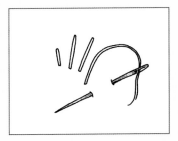

Straight stitch

This is a single stitch that can be worked in varying lengths. It is useful for embroidering short lines.

Cross stitch

1 Bring the needle through to the front of the work, then take the first stitch diagonally from right to left, bringing the needle back through in line with the point where the first stitch emerged.

2 Complete the cross stitch by inserting the needle back through the work in line with the top of the previous stitch, from right to left.

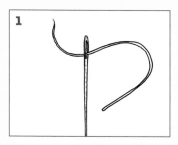

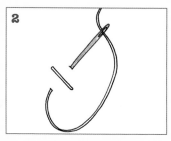

Pompoms

The rabbit's tail is crocheted incorporating loops of chain stitches. A fluffy pompom can be made as a simple alternative.

1 Cut two circles of cardboard to the required measurement for the pompom. Make a hole in the center of each circle. The hole should be around a third of the size of the finished pompom. Thread a blunt needle with a long length of doubled yarn and, with the two circles of cardboard together, wind the yarn through the hole and around the outer edge of the circle. Continue in this way, using new lengths of yarn until the hole is filled and the circle is covered.

2 Cut through the yarn around the outer edge between the two circles of cardboard. Tie a length of yarn securely around the middle, leaving long ends with which to attach the pompom. Remove the cardboard and trim the pompom, fluffing it into shape.

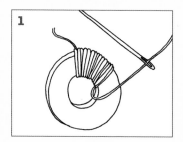

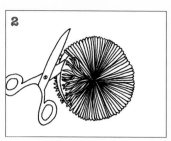

Back stitch

With right sides together, begin by working a couple of stitches over each other to secure the seam. Bring the needle through to the front of the work one stitch ahead of the last stitch made. Then insert the needle back through the work at the end of the last stitch. Repeat to complete the seam, making sure your stitches are neat and worked in a straight line.

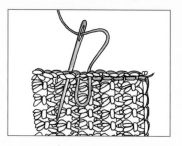

Safety issues with babies and young children

Care should be taken if crocheting these projects for babies and children under three years of age. Do not use yarns that are prone to shedding loose fibers, and ensure that all seams are stitched securely. Buttons and beads should not be used for eyes. French knots can be embroidered on the snake, fox, and monkey instead. The buttons used for the eyes of the deer can be replaced with crocheted discs, which should be securely sewn in place.

To make ⅜in (1cm)-diameter eye

Using Sport-weight yarn and B/1–C/2 hook, wind yarn around a finger a couple of times to form a ring, insert the hook, catch the yarn and draw back through the ring.
Next: Work 6 sc into the ring. Sl st to next st and fasten off. Pull on short end of yarn to close ring. Sew in place to the face of the crocheted animal.

Abbreviations

ch	chain
cm	centimeter(s)
cont	continue
dc	double crochet
dec	decrease
dtr	double treble
hdc	half double crochet
in	inch(es)
inc	increase
LHS	left-hand side
rem	remaining
rep	repeat
RHS	right-hand side
RS	right side
sc	single crochet
sc2tog	work 2 single crochet stitches together to decrease
sk	skip
sl st	slip stitch
sp	space
st(s)	stitch(es)
tr	treble
WS	wrong side
yo	yarn over

Conversions

Steel crochet hook conversion

Metric (mm)	UK:	US:
0.60	6	14
0.70	–	13
0.75	5	12
–	4½	11
1.00	4	10
–	3½	9
1.25	3	8
1.50	2½	7
1.75	2	6
–	1½	5

Aluminum crochet hook conversion

Metric (mm)	UK:	US:
2.00	14	–
2.25	13	B/1
2.50	12	–
2.75	–	C/2
3.00	11	–
3.25	10	D/3
3.50	9	E/4
3.75	–	F/5
4.00	8	G/6
4.50	7	7
5.00	6	H/8
5.50	5	I/9
6.00	4	J/10
6.50	3	K/10½
7.00	2	–
8.00	0	L/11
9.00	00	M/13
10.00	000	N/15
11.50	–	P/16

techniques

Suppliers

YARNS

Below are listed the contact details for the yarn manufacturers whose yarns are used for the projects in this book. Many of them ship to the US or list the details of US-based distributors and retailers of their yarn lines.

Adriafil
Via Coriano 58,
47924 Rimini, Italy
Tel: +39 (0) 541 383 706
www.adriafil.com

Bergère de France
55020 Bar-le-duc Cedex, France
Tel: +33 (0) 329 793 666
www.bergeredefrance.com

Deramores
Units 5–9 Tomas Seth Business Park, Argent Road
Queenborough ME11 5TS, UK
Tel: +44 (0) 8455 194 573
www.deramores.com

King Cole
Merrie Mills, Elliott Street
Silsden
West Yorkshire BD20 0DE, UK
Tel: +44 (0) 1535 650 230
www.kingcole.co.uk

Patons
320 Livingstone Avenue South
Box 40, Listowel, ON N4W 3H3, Canada
Tel: +1 888 368 8401
www.patonsyarns.com

Rico Design
Industriestr. 19–23
33034 Brakel, Germany
Tel: +49 (0) 52 72 602-0
www.rico-design.de

Rowan Yarns
Green Lane Mill
Holmfirth
West Yorkshire HD9 2DX, UK
Tel: +44 (0) 1484 681 881
www.knitrowan.com

Sirdar Spinning Ltd
Flanshaw Lane
Wakefield
West Yorkshire WF2 9ND, UK
Tel: +44 (0) 1924 231 682
www.sirdar.co.uk

If you are unable to source the specific brand of yarn specified, you may wish to substitute a yarn that is readily available at your local yarn shop or at retail stores such as Hobby Lobby, Jo-Ann fabric and craft stores, Michael's stores, Target, and Wal-Mart. See also page 148 for advice on substituing yarns.

Find your local yarn shop:
www.sweaterbabe.com/directory
www.knitmap.com
www.yarngroup.org

Hobby Lobby
www.hobbylobby.com

Jo-Ann fabric and craft stores
www.joann.com

Michael's stores
www.michaels.com

Target
www.Target.com

Wal-Mart
www.walmart.com

If you are substituting brands of yarn, be sure to do a gauge swatch. Yarn companies Bernat, Caron, Lion Brand Yarn, Patons, and Red Heart all offer helpful information on yarn substitution.

Bernat
www.bernat.com

Caron
www.caron.com

Lion Brand Yarn
www.lionbrand.com

Patons
www.patonsyarns.com

Red Heart
www.redheart.com

HOOKS
Purl Soho
459 Broome Street
New York, NY 10013
Tel: +1 212 420 8796
www.purlsoho.com

HABERDASHERY
Brooklyn General Store
128 Union Street
Brooklyn, NY 11231
Tel: +1 718 237 7753
www.brooklyngeneral.com

EMBROIDERY THREADS
DMC
The DMC Corporation
10 Basin Drive, Suite 130
Kearny, NJ 07032
Tel: +1 973 589 0606
www.dmc-usa.com

BEADS
MK Beads
618 SW 3rd St #150
Cape Coral, FL 33991
Tel: +1 239 634 2232
www.mkbeads.com

BATTING AND STUFFING
Fabric and Art
101 Boatyard Drive
Fort Bragg, CA 95437
Tel: +1 707 964 6365
www.fabricandart.com

About the author

Vanessa Mooncie is a contemporary crochet jewelry designer and maker, silkscreen artist, and illustrator. She spent many happy hours as a child learning to crochet and knit with her mother and grandmother. She went on to study fashion and textile design, then became a children's wear designer, illustrator, and commercial interior designer. She lives with her family in the English countryside.

Acknowledgments

I would like to thank Jonathan Bailey for giving me the great opportunity to do *Crocheted Wild Animals*. Thank you to Wendy McAngus for all your patience and support, and many thanks to the editor, Nicola Hodgson, and to all at GMC. For their continuous encouragement, I thank my husband Damian, my daughters Miriam, Dilys, Honey, and granddaughter Dolly, and a special thank you to my son, Flynn, who gave me the idea for the reversible chameleon, which I am particularly proud of!

Index

To place an order, or to request a catalog, contact
The Taunton Press, Inc.
63 South Main Street, P.O. Box 5506, Newtown, CT 06470-5506
www.taunton.com